PRAISE FOR AMBER + RYE

"It is such a joy to finally see a cookbook on beautiful Baltic cuisine, done with so much sensitivity and respect by Zuza Zak, one of my favorite authors. It is making me pine to travel to the region more than ever. Before I can do that, I will enjoy reading and cooking from this wonderful book."

OLIA HERCULES, *SUMMER KITCHENS*

"Beautifully written and thoroughly researched, Zuza Zak's new book offers a warmly personal insight into a vibrant cuisine of the little-known region of the Baltic states. Zuza's passion for the history, the folklore, and the cuisine shines through, making *Amber & Rye* more than just a recipe book. It is a beautiful portrait of the region—its landscape, its history, its people, and of course its food. Ranging from familiar Soviet-era classics to unique regional and modern gems, the recipes are versatile, exciting, inviting, and full of flavor. This book is a real highlight within the culinary travelogue genre!"

ALISSA TIMOSHKINA, *SALT & TIME: RECIPES FROM A RUSSIAN KITCHEN*

"Zuza has an enchanting way with recipe names and her flavor combinations are irresistible. Chanterelles & blueberries, Fermented beet elixir, Kaja's "sour milk lady" with berries, Kama yogurt with plum butter. This is food to fit with the fairytale landscapes the book describes."

ELEANOR FORD, *FIRE ISLANDS*

"Zuza Zak deftly steers us from place to plate though the Baltic trisect of countries, Estonia, Latvia, and Lithuania, in her illuminating *Amber & Rye*, a cookbook brimming with approachable recipes and mouth-watering photographs."

CAROLINE EDEN, *BLACK SEA*

"Zuza Zak is truly the best ambassador for Eastern European culture and cuisine. This book is full of reach-in-and-grab photographs of both food on plates, but also recognizable ingredients full of nostalgia and *toska*. There's a sense of abundance and generosity in Zuza's writing, her storytelling and in the food itself. This book is as much a traveler's guide as it is a cook's compendium of Baltic cuisine."

ALICE ZASLAVSKY, *IN PRAISE OF VEG*

Honeycombs, rye ears, rue, tulips and lilies.
Lazy, sweet-toothed bears. Pine resin—golden amber,
Baltic foam slowly dissolving into the amber sand.

FROM *WHITE SHROUD*, BY ANTANAS ŠKĖMA

ZUZA ZAK

AMBER & RYE
A BALTIC FOOD JOURNEY
Estonia ✳ Latvia ✳ Lithuania

Interlink Books

An imprint of Interlink Publishing Group, Inc.
Northampton, Massachusetts

For *my daughters*

CONTENTS

MY BALTIC ODYSSEY

It all began, as adventures often do, with a story. When I was growing up in Warsaw, my Grandma Halinka would talk endlessly about her idyllic childhood in Lithuania. In painstaking detail, Halinka described to me the dreamy days of her youth, the places she loved in and around Vilnius, and the people who lived there. She brought it all so vividly to life that I sometimes felt as if I'd been there with her, and would ask her to remind me of some person or detail I'd forgotten, or just wanted to hear about again. Her polished mahogany wardrobe, filled to the brim with shiny brooches, leather gloves, multicolored scarves and golden-hued amber necklaces was like a secret doorway to that enchanted world of my imagination.

Halinka belonged to an entire generation in exile, people from the Kresy strip of Poland ("the borderlands" that became Soviet territory after World War II) who were destined to spend their lives pining for the lost lands of their youth.

Then, a couple of years ago, my dad was given a DNA test as a Christmas present, and the results revealed him to be half-Balt, half-Polish. As my grandmother came from Lithuania, this may not seem so surprising; however, she had always maintained that her family were of exclusively Polish heritage. Perplexed, I decided to delve deeper, and discovered that many people who identified as Poles living in Lithuania were in fact ethnically Lithuanian—and therefore Balt. For many years a *Gente lituanus, natione polonus* ("Lithuanian tribe, Polish nation") mentality had prevailed, meaning that despite being deeply connected to Lithuania, people like my grandmother considered themselves to be Polish. Perhaps this explained her pain at being separated from not only the land of her childhood but also that of her ancestors.

The Polish Baltic coast of my own childhood memories was a feast for the senses: long walks through shady forests heady with the scent of pines (still to this day my favorite smell) before emerging into the blinding light of white, powdered-sugar-soft sand underfoot. Jumping in the frothy waves—translucent and freezing, rarely calm. Since the coastline was so far from my home in Warsaw, we did not go there often, and as a result, it became engraved on my memory. Food took on a special significance in this setting. There was the daily pilgrimage to a beach shack—usually a concrete block in Eastern Europe—for fish soup; tubes of rich, sweet condensed milk to suck on (just as a snack!); waffles covered in fluffy whipped cream; overflowing ice-cream cones at sunset; and evenings brought sausages sizzling over a fire on the beach.

An urge to get to know more of this magical coastline, together with my recently discovered genetic link with the Baltics, prompted me to explore further.

A BRIEF BALTIC HISTORY

Initially used in the Germanic languages as a collective name for the countries fringing the Baltic Sea, the modern term 'Baltic States' was coined to reflect the new-found independence of Estonia, Latvia, and Lithuania after World War II. Although these countries have similarities that bring them together, there are also notable differences. And if language reflects our perspective on the world, then Baltic mindsets must be quite distinct from one another. While Lithuanian is among the oldest languages in the world, comparable to Sanskrit and ancient Greek (some say it's made for poetry), Latvian has undergone rapid development and modernization (like English, it's constantly changing). Estonian, meanwhile, is closer to Finnish than it is to the languages of its Baltic neighbors.

The geographical positioning of the Baltic States, with their strategic advantage of access to the Baltic Sea, means that their territory has frequently been encroached upon. Baltic Germans arrived in Latvia and Estonia in the thirteenth century and would remain in the region for the best part of 700 years, so their impact cannot be overstated. In Estonia, they quickly became the ruling elite, with the German language taking precedence; in Lithuania, on the other hand, they helped local rulers establish towns including Vilnius, the modern-day capital.

In the late fourteenth century, the Polish queen Jadwiga married the Lithuanian grand duke Jagiełło, heralding a prosperous time in both of their countries, and paving the way for the formation of the Polish-Lithuanian Commonwealth in 1569. An ethnically diverse territory, the commonwealth spanned most of Eastern Europe, from southern Estonia to northern Moldova, but over the next two centuries its power weakened considerably.

To the east, Russia has been a constant presence: in the sixteenth century, Estonia was invaded by Ivan the Terrible before his forces were defeated by the combined might of Sweden and the Polish-Lithuanian Commonwealth. Baltic nobles swore allegiance to the Swedish crown, and grammar and religious books were published in the Estonian language for the first time. Such cultural progress, however, was soon halted by famine and the twenty-one-year Great Northern War, which ended in 1721 with a victorious Russia seizing power in the Baltics.

Only after World War I was independence regained by the Baltic States. This joy was short-lived, however, with Soviet forces occupying Estonia, Latvia, and Lithuania following World War II. Swallowed by the USSR, local culture was subjugated once again, and the Russian language now dominated. It can be difficult to convey the oppression and absurdity of living under such a regime to those who haven't experienced it—but an episode recounted by Epp Annus, an Estonian researcher at the University of Ohio, gives an insight into everyday life during this era. In the 1950s, when her parents were a young couple, they were picking mushrooms in the forest on a warm September's day. However, when they came across two armed Soviet soldiers, the soldiers brusquely fired questions at them in Russian and demanded to see identity documents. Her parents had not thought to bring their documents with them, so they were taken in and held.

Over the course of the day, many more young people, "caught out" in the forest without documents, joined them. Entertaining themselves by playing ball games, they waited for hours, until finally, they were all released, given back their mushrooms, and sent home.

During these strange times in the Baltics, music became a battleground, with the Soviets using folk music to extol the virtues of their idols and changing the lyrics to suit their purposes—but in the late 1980s a counter-movement emerged, using authentic folk music as a symbol of freedom and a way of forging a connection to something deeper. This became known as the Singing Revolution and culminated in the formation of the Baltic Way, a two-million-strong human chain that stretched from Tallinn to Vilnius.

The momentum of this campaign is widely thought to have contributed to the dissolution of the Soviet Union in 1989.

Following the fall of the Iron Curtain, and in the wake of the revolutions that rippled across Eastern Europe, the Baltic States were faced with a new set of economic and social challenges, which they have dealt with in various ways.

In Lithuania, an inclusive policy towards minorities—mainly Russian settlers, but also many Poles—has instilled a sense of belonging, while Estonia has taken steps to foster greater economic equality.

Although the region's history has been difficult at times, while traveling in the Baltics I was left with the distinct impression that Estonia, Latvia, and Lithuania are forging a bright future—one in which its culture, from its love of music and the arts, to its food traditions, is a celebration of hard-won freedom and individuality.

THE JOURNEY BEGINS

With my grandmother's stories ringing in my ears, and my own precious memories of long-ago holidays spent on the Baltic coast, I had a feeling that treasures deeply connected to the past were waiting to be discovered. I decided to set off on my very own odyssey of amber: as a food writer, my "Baltic gold" was to be culinary treasure, rather than the golden resin that washes up on Baltic shores and that so intrigued the ancient civilizations.

Plans were duly made. I would be traveling with my three-year-old daughter, Nusia, and my partner, Yasin, who was going to photograph the trip. Before heading off on our Baltic odyssey, I had imagined a region that was Nordic in its moods: unpredictable, with dark forests and a grey sea. This climate is one reason why winter-hardy rye is such an important crop in the Baltics, and has been for more than a thousand years. Yet during our summertime sojourn we experienced long balmy days, beautiful golden light, and sunsets that lasted late into the evening. Fields of rye shimmered as we drove past; it was like something out of a fairytale.

Everything happened at the right time and effortlessly. In Estonia, when we drove to a fish restaurant in the harbor at Neeme, our waiter turned out to be the son of novelist and poet Kai Aareleid, and he regaled us with his mother's writing and experiences; when we arrived in Karuse, it coincided with a festival celebrating local food traditions, with farms, houses, and galleries in nearby villages reopening as impromptu cafes for the evening.

There, deep in the forest, we met Meelike, who lived in a disused railway station she had lovingly renovated, creating a magical world of wild mushrooms, berries, and goats—one that embraced a simple, blissful way of life, in harmony with nature. Meelike introduced us to a local superwoman, Mirjam. As well as raising three young children, Mirjam runs Mätiku organic dairy farm in nearby Oidrema and drives the new Baltic food movement forward, inspiring producers to share family recipes. She also teaches in the community and exchanges ideas with others across Europe—it was Mirjam who encouraged her neighbors, Kaja and Urmas, to start a business making traditional Estonian sausages from their kitchen.

Armed with Mirjam's map of farmers, growers, and artisan producers across the Baltics, I was able to meet many of the people behind this "new wave" of Baltic food.

Tomorrow morning we'll cut the rye,
We'll cut the rye and bind it into sheaves,
When we stack them up, when we bind them up,
The field will resound when we sing,
When we stack them up, when we bind them up,
The field will resound when we sing.

TRADITIONAL LITHUANIAN FOLK SONG

*Exploring the diverse landscapes of the Baltic States,
I found a wonderland of golden seashores, dappled
forests, friendly goats, and farmhouse kitchens,
where I was warmly welcomed and well fed.*

EXPLORING BALTIC FOOD & CULTURE: THE "NEW WAVE"

Like many of us in our globalized world, the people of the Baltic States eat food from all over. Ever since Estonia, Latvia, and Lithuania joined the European Union in 2004, international trends have become more influential. With chefs free to immerse themselves in various cuisines, in Baltic cities you can now find everything from bao buns filled with chanterelles to Tex-Mex standards accompanied by enormous tequila cocktails.

However, while new styles of cooking are informed by time spent abroad and an openness towards other cultures and cuisines, there is also a revival of ancient Baltic ways, old recipes, and local, seasonal ingredients. Although each nation has its own traditional dishes, this emerging food movement is broad enough to encompass regionality and allow the Baltic States to create something together, not through uniformity, but in a way that celebrates their individual food cultures.

This food renaissance has gone hand in hand with a wider cultural revival, as the region shrugs off what I like to describe as "the Communist hangover." Because of my own experience of the grey Communist days in 1980s Poland, I feel a deep joy at the unstoppable spread of vigor and inspiration in places that have endured hardship—it is fundamentally life-affirming. When I watched Pawel Pawlikowski's film *Cold War*, set in Communist Poland, I understood why it had to be made in black and white. As a child growing up in Warsaw, I don't remember much color: a bright-yellow banana was not only a rare treat, but also conveyed a sense of freedom and the bounty of the West.

Yet, looking back, I can see the appeal of the strong, brutalist aesthetic of the era. And with the passage of time, there is now a younger generation with no memory of those days who can view this recent history from a new perspective. Consequently, the Soviet era is being reinterpreted, in literature as well as in food, and Soviet-style food is starting to be remembered with a touch of nostalgia.

INTO THE KITCHEN

Just as the ocean's waves are a foretaste of the deep blue beyond, so a region's food reflects something more profound than its obvious, everyday aspect. Through the simple act of cooking and eating, we can gain access to another culture. I am always touched when strangers open their homes and hearts to me. It's one thing eating a beautifully prepared meal in a restaurant, but quite another being in someone else's home, exchanging stories and feeling the warmth of hospitality. The Baltic restaurant and the Baltic home are two different worlds, yet their aim is the same: preserving heritage. In creating the recipes for this book, I have been greatly inspired by both.

My aim is to take you on a journey of discovery through this emerging cuisine, and to share the unforgettable stories and culture of the people who live in the Baltic region.

The creativity and passion I saw there was contagious and it fired my own ideas, so while the recipes here are based on Baltic cuisine, they are not entirely traditional. I wanted to write an inclusive cookbook, in the spirit of the Baltic States: I was determined that it would be accessible to any home cook willing to try something new, because I believe that Baltic food has something to offer everyone, vegans included (vegan, vegetarian, and pescatarian recipes are flagged throughout).

The cuisines of Estonia, Latvia, and Lithuania have undergone a renaissance in recent years, creating a cooking style that is modern and exciting. Dubbed "new Nordic" by some, to my mind it lies somewhere between Slavic Eastern Europe and Scandinavia, with its unique Baltic spirit firmly anchoring it in time and place. This is the spirit I wanted to capture within the pages of this book.

BEGINNINGS

That cozy feeling when a bowl of porridge warms your cold-weary bones; sharing one too many sweet pastries and coffee refills across a table with friends; Bloody Marys and eggs on sourdough doused with Tabasco, eaten in silence, after a night out. Breakfast has always been my favorite meal. There is little I love more in life than sitting down to a leisurely breakfast of nourishing grains, runny eggs, seasonal fruit, and flaky pastries. Whether you prefer to start your day sweet or savory, or both, in this chapter you'll find original breakfast and brunch ideas inspired by the flavors of the Baltic. Some are perfect for a quick and easy weekday breakfast, others are more suitable for drawn-out brunches with friends and family. In particular, I hope you will try typically Estonian *kama* (so wholesome) and hemp butter from Latvia (addictive!) as well as my own take on some Eastern European classics, such as *syrniki* pancakes and *manna* porridge.

I find hemp butter addictive: it's like a crunchier, earthier, healthier peanut butter, sort of. It can be used in both sweet and savory dishes and is naturally vegan. I like to eat it while it's still warm on sourdough toast (or rye crispbreads) drizzled with wildflower honey. And if no good honey is on hand, I have been known to douse it in condensed milk instead—heaven!

Hemp butter only takes about 10 minutes to make once you've got your hands on some unhulled hemp seeds and hempseed oil (see page 245); it's worth noting, however, that in some countries, unhulled hemp seeds are impossible to get hold of, even illegal—in which case, you can replace them with the hulled variety, perhaps adding a little salt too. The resulting hemp butter will be lighter and less crunchy, but just as delicious; some may even prefer this milder version.

HEMP BUTTER & HONEY ON TOAST

SERVES 4

* 4 slices sourdough bread
* Generous 1 tablespoon wildflower or other good honey

For the hemp butter

* Generous 1 cup (200 g) unhulled hemp seeds
* 2½ tablespoons hempseed oil

VEGAN

Toast the hemp seeds in a dry frying pan over medium heat for 7–8 minutes or until they smell nutty, stirring often. Tip the seeds into a powerful food processor and blend, scraping the sides down every so often, until you have a damp, powdery paste. Slowly pour in the oil and keep blending until it turns into one mass (the texture is meant to be crunchy).

Toast the bread, spread with the freshly made, still-warm hemp butter, and drizzle some beautiful honey over the top. Enjoy.

Stored in a sterilized screw-top jar (see page 178 for my preferred sterilizing method). The rest of the hemp butter will keep for a few months, though it never seems to last that long in my house.

Syrniki are pancakes made from *twaróg* (curd cheese) and eaten in many guises all over the Baltic States. They are often served for breakfast topped with sour cream and berries, but once I'd eaten them with chocolate buckwheat, there was no going back. The trick to making them fluffy, I find, is to use an extra soft, fine flour, but if none is available, all-purpose will be fine. You can buy roasted buckwheat (*kasza gryczana*) and *twaróg* cheese from Polish food shops.

SYRNIKI PANCAKES
WITH SUMMER BERRY SALAD & CHOCOLATE BUCKWHEAT

SERVES 4

* 10½ oz (300 g) *twaróg* or farmer cheese
* 2 eggs, lightly beaten
* ¼ teaspoon salt
* 4 tablespoons 00 pasta flour or all-purpose flour
* 2 tablespoons sugar
* 1 teaspoon vanilla extract
* Rapeseed oil, for frying
* Sour cream or crème fraîche, to serve

For the summer berry salad

* 7 oz (200 g) mixed berries, such as blackberries, raspberries, and quartered strawberries
* Handful of torn mint leaves
* Marigold flowers—optional

For the chocolate buckwheat

* 2 tablespoons roasted buckwheat (kasha)
* 1 tablespoon butter
* 1 tablespoon honey
* 1 tablespoon cacao powder

VEGETARIAN

For the summer berry salad, combine the berries with the mint. If you are using marigold flowers, pull off some of the petals and mix them into the salad, saving a few whole flowers for decoration. Set aside.

In a large bowl, use a fork to mash the cheese and eggs with the salt. Add half of the flour and sugar and all of the vanilla extract and carry on mashing until all the ingredients are well combined (if you are using *twaróg*, the mixture will retain some texture). Cover and leave to chill in the fridge while you make the chocolate buckwheat.

Pour about 2 tablespoons of oil into a heavy-based frying pan over medium heat. Add the buckwheat and cook, stirring, for about 2 minutes, until it smells nutty and has turned a shade darker. In a saucepan, melt the butter with the honey, then stir in the cacao powder. Using a slotted spoon, scoop out the buckwheat and drain on paper towels. Tip into a heatproof bowl and pour the butter, honey, and cacao mixture on top. Stir well, then allow to cool while you cook the *syrniki*.

Preheat the oven to 200°F (100°C). Scatter the remaining flour over a plate. Form tablespoonfuls of the *syrniki* mixture into balls, then roll in the flour. Heat a film of oil in a large non-stick frying pan over medium heat. Working in batches, fry the *syrniki* for 3–4 minutes on each side until golden brown. Drain on paper towels, then keep warm in the oven while you cook the rest.

Serve with the chocolate buckwheat, sour cream or crème fraîche, and plenty of summer berry salad. Decorate with the reserved marigold flowers, if using.

We saw those berries, over-ripe and glowing,
in weak and tepid light of the October sun
persisting red as blood in right full growing,
without much inkling of the winter clouds to come...

FROM *QUESTION*, BY MARIE UNDER

He had enjoyed the waffles. Nevertheless, those crunchy pastries topped with custard were making Teedu inexplicably disturbed at the moment. This feeling had nothing to do with the waffles as a baked good, naturally, but rather with what they symbolized.

FROM *THE CAVEMEN CHRONICLE*,
BY MIHKEL MUTT

Waffles being construed as a symbol of Estonian independence must rank among my favorite moments in Baltic literature! Having spent my childhood in Communist Poland, I completely understand how the sort of things we take for granted in the West can be highly significant in a place where food isn't always easy to come by. For the cowardly Teedu, who always towed the party line, waffles signified a disturbing development; for other, more endearing characters in the book, they were a sign of great things to come ...

In this recipe, I simply had to pair the waffles with that most Estonian of foods, *kama*—a mixture of ground grains that is most often eaten at breakfast time—and zingy sea buckthorn. If you can't source sea buckthorn, feel free to use blueberries or raspberries instead.

INDEPENDENCE WAFFLES
WITH KAMA CREAM & SEA BUCKTHORN

SERVES 4

* Generous ¾ cup (200 ml) heavy whipping cream
* 2 tablespoons confectioners' sugar
* 4 tablespoons *kama* (see page 36)
* Handful of sea buckthorn berries (see page 246) or other tart berries

For the waffle batter

* 1⅔ cups (200 g) all-purpose flour
* 1¼ cups (300 ml) whole milk
* 2 teaspoons baking powder
* 1 teaspoon sugar
* 1 egg
* ½ teaspoon vanilla extract

VEGETARIAN

Make the waffle batter by whisking all the ingredients together in a bowl or jug until smooth and lump-free. Allow the batter to stand for 10 minutes before using.

Meanwhile, whip the cream to soft peaks. Add the confectioners' sugar and mix until completely combined, then stir in the *kama*.

Cook the batter in a waffle maker, following the manufacturer's instructions. (If you don't have a waffle maker, I suggest making fluffy pancakes instead. You can use the outside of a small round cake pan placed inside the frying pan to create a perfect circle. Melt a tiny bit of butter in the middle and pour in half a ladleful of the batter. Cook over medium heat for a couple of minutes or until set around the edges, then carefully remove the pan and flip the pancake over to brown on the other side.)

Serve the waffles (or pancakes) topped with the *kama* cream and sea buckthorn or other berries.

Smooth, silky semolina porridge makes a wonderful alternative to oatmeal, and it takes no extra time to cook. Warm *manna* porridge (*manna* simply means semolina, but the term also denotes the fineness of the grain) very quickly develops a skin on top, so you can be creative with toppings and sauces. I like to top it with stewed seasonal fruit—that way, it can also double as a dessert once it cools. If you want to try birch syrup, you can order it online (see page 245), otherwise you could just use maple syrup instead.

SPICED CACAO MANNA PORRIDGE

SERVES 2–3

- ¼ cup (40 g) fine semolina
- 2 tablespoons cacao powder
- ½ teaspoon ground cinnamon
- ½ teaspoon ground cardamom
- 2 tablespoons birch or maple syrup, plus extra for drizzling
- 2½ cups (600 ml) whole milk
- 1 egg yolk
- Thickened cream or crème fraîche and strawberries, to serve

VEGETARIAN

In a large cup or small bowl, combine the semolina with the cacao powder, spices, birch or maple syrup, and half of the milk. Mix to a smooth paste.

Heat the remainder of the milk in a saucepan until small bubbles begin to appear, then turn the heat right down and pour in the semolina paste, while stirring constantly. Start with a wooden spoon, but if the porridge starts to look lumpy and is thickening very fast, grab a hand whisk and give it a vigorous whisking. When the porridge starts to thicken, whisk in the egg yolk.

Once you have a smooth porridge of the consistency you like, pour into bowls and allow to stand for a moment. Drizzle with syrup and serve with cream or crème fraîche and strawberries.

Potato-hash pancakes—or *latkes* in Yiddish—are known as a traditional part of Jewish cuisine. It's not surprising, therefore, that they are also commonplace in Lithuanian cooking, since Lithuania (like many Eastern European countries) had a huge Jewish community prior to World War II. For hundreds of years, recipes, ingredients, and techniques were shared in a way that makes tracing their origins impossible; luckily, it's also unnecessary. Likewise, I find it unnecessary to peel the potatoes unless they are looking a bit worse for wear.

Some may find the *kiełbasa* sausage a surprising addition here, given the Jewish name of this dish, but it's delicious! You can, of course, use kosher sausage instead, if you prefer.

POTATO LATKES
WITH SMOKED SAUSAGE & SPINACH

SERVES 4

* 1¾ oz (50 g) smoked *kiełbasa*-style sausage, cubed
* 7 oz (200 g) spinach leaves
* Squeeze of lemon juice
* Salt and black pepper

For the latkes
* 2 medium potatoes
* 2 French shallots, finely chopped
* 1 egg, lightly beaten
* 2 tablespoons all-purpose flour
* Rapeseed oil, for frying

Preheat the oven to 200°F (100°C).

For the *latkes*, coarsely grate the potatoes into a large bowl. Add the shallots, egg, and flour and mix well. Season generously with salt and pepper.

Heat a thin film of oil in a large frying pan over medium heat. Once it's hot, add tablespoonfuls of the potato mixture to the pan, working in batches and taking care not to overcrowd the pan. Flatten the *latkes* with your fork and fry for about 2–3 minutes on the first side, until golden, then flip and cook for another 2–3 minutes on the other side. Drain the cooked *latkes* on paper towels and keep warm in the oven.

Add a little more oil to the frying pan and add the sausage. Fry until it crisps up, then add the spinach. Once the spinach has wilted (this will only take a minute or so), add a squeeze of lemon juice and season with salt and pepper.

Serve the sausage and spinach on top of the *latkes*.

Usually when you make something with yeast it's best to eat it there and then, or at least the same day. However, these pumpkin buns are an exception. I have eaten them with great pleasure the next day and even the day after that! I think the secret may lie in the moisture the pumpkin adds to the dough and the filling, which helps to keep them soft.

PILLOWY PUMPKIN BUNS

MAKES 12–14

* 1 oz (25 g) fresh yeast or ½ oz (15 g) active-dry yeast
* Scant ½ cup (100 ml) whole milk, warmed
* 2 tablespoons sugar
* 4 cups (500 g) all-purpose flour
* ½ teaspoon salt
* 1 cup (250 g) Pumpkin puree (see page 186)
* 1 egg, lightly beaten
* 5½ tablespoons (80 g) unsalted butter, melted
* 1 egg yolk, for glazing
* 2 tablespoons pumpkin seeds (pepitas)

For the filling

* 7 oz (200 g) *twaróg* or farmer cheese
* 3 tablespoons Pumpkin puree (see page 186)
* 2 tablespoons sugar
* ½ teaspoon ground cinnamon
* ½ teaspoon ground cardamom
* A couple of gratings of nutmeg—optional

VEGETARIAN

First of all, in a jug or small bowl, combine the yeast with the milk, sugar, and a tablespoon of the flour. Leave somewhere warm to activate for 20 minutes, or until frothy.

In a large bowl, use your hands to combine the rest of the flour with the salt, pumpkin puree, and egg. Add the yeast mixture and start to bring the dough together—it will be sticky at this point, but try not to add any more flour if you can help it. Pour in the melted butter, which should help you gather the dough into a ball. Cover the bowl with a clean tea towel, and leave the dough in a warm place to rise for 40–50 minutes or until doubled in size.

Meanwhile, make the filling by mashing all the ingredients together with a fork. Set aside.

Preheat the oven to 350°F (180°C) and line a large baking sheet with parchment paper.

Turn the dough out onto a floured surface and knead for about 10 minutes. I'm told it's good to "beat up" this kind of dough, so don't be afraid to be a little rough!

Evenly divide the dough into 12–14 balls. Flatten each one into a circle about 1½ inches (4 cm) across and place a heaped teaspoonful of filling in the center. Bring the edges up and over the filling and seal by pressing together.

Place the buns on the baking sheet, spacing them out since they will expand in the oven. Glaze with egg yolk, sprinkle with pumpkin seeds, and bake for 30 minutes until risen and golden brown.

If you wake up feeling dull and jaded, there's only one thing for it: these buns! First you will need to forage for elderflowers—in itself, a magically life-affirming act. Then there's the yeasty smell that will permeate your kitchen, and once you finally take a bite you'll be won over by the soft, sticky texture and uncannily fragrant, mellow sweetness of the filling. If elderflower season is over, use a scant ½ cup (100 ml) store-bought elderflower syrup instead of making the syrup for the filling, and if there are no peaches, try substituting pears. If you don't feel like messing around making a filling at all, just use your favorite jam.

FRAGRANT ELDERFLOWER & PEACH BREAKFAST BUNS

MAKES 6–8

- 1 oz (25 g) fresh yeast or ½ oz (15 g) dried yeast
- ¼ cup (50 g) sugar
- Scant ½ cup (100 ml) whole milk, warmed
- 1⅔ cups (200 g) all-purpose flour, plus extra for dusting
- Pinch of salt
- 1½ tablespoons (25 g) butter, melted
- 1 egg yolk, lightly beaten

For the filling

- 10 elderflower heads, washed under running water
- 3 tablespoons superfine sugar
- 1 teaspoon finely grated lemon zest
- 2 peaches, pitted and chopped
- ½ teaspoon vanilla extract
- 1 teaspoon cornstarch

For the crumble topping

- 1 tablespoon brown sugar
- 1 tablespoon all-purpose flour
- 1 tablespoon butter
- Pinch of ground cinnamon

VEGETARIAN

For the filling, put the elderflower heads in a stainless steel saucepan with the sugar and lemon zest. Cover with a generous ¾ cup (200 ml) of water and bring to a boil, stirring until the sugar dissolves, then turn the heat down to low and simmer for about 15 minutes—it's ready when your house is filled with the fragrance of elderflowers! Turn off the heat and leave to cool and infuse for 10 minutes before straining through a fine sieve, discarding the elderflowers. Return the syrup to the pan, add the peaches, and bring to a boil again, then turn the heat right down and simmer for about 10 minutes or until the fruit has disintegrated. Add the vanilla extract and sift in the cornstarch. Stir constantly for about 10 minutes until the filling thickens, then turn the heat off and allow to cool.

In a large mixing bowl, combine the yeast with the sugar and milk and leave to activate in a warm place for 20 minutes or until frothy. Sift the flour and salt into the yeast mixture and mix with one hand, while slowly pouring in the melted butter, to make a rough dough. Turn out of the bowl onto a flour-dusted surface and knead for 5–10 minutes until smooth and elastic. Cover the bowl with a clean tea towel and leave the dough to rise in a warm place for 45–50 minutes or until doubled in size.

Preheat the oven to 350°F (180°C) and lightly grease an 8-inch (20 cm) round cake pan.

Tip the dough out onto a floured surface and punch down, then use a rolling pin to roll it out into a rectangle about ½ inch (1 cm) thick. Spread with the filling, leaving a ¾-inch (2 cm) border all around the edges and, starting from one of the longer sides, roll up the dough. Cut the roll evenly into 6–8 slices and arrange them snugly, cut sides up, in the cake pan. Cover with the tea towel and allow to rise for 20 minutes or until they fill the pan.

Make the crumble topping by rubbing together all of the ingredients with your fingertips until the mixture resembles breadcrumbs.

Gently brush the risen buns with egg yolk, then sprinkle with the crumble topping and bake for 25 minutes until golden.

Considering the amount of both pastries and sea buckthorn I saw—and ate—in my travels around the Baltic States, I was a bit sad not to come across them together. On my return home, I decided to put things right and so developed this simple recipe to unite two Baltic favorites. The sea buckthorn berries give a pleasant tang to the sweet crumbly pastry, but this could instead be added by other tart berries, such as raspberries or blackberries.

SEA BUCKTHORN PASTRIES

MAKES 12–16

* 2½ cups (300 g) all-purpose flour, plus extra for dusting
* 1 teaspoon salt
* 2¼ sticks (250 g) cold unsalted butter
* Squeeze of lemon juice
* Generous ¾ cup (200 ml) chilled water

For the custard topping

* Generous ¾ cup (200 ml) whole milk
* Scant ½ cup (100 ml) heavy cream
* 1 vanilla bean, split lengthways
* 2 egg yolks
* 3 tablespoons sugar
* 2 teaspoons cornstarch
* Ice
* Handful of sea buckthorn berries (see page 246)
* 1 tablespoon dark brown sugar

VEGETARIAN

Combine the flour and salt in a large mixing bowl, then grate in the butter, stirring it in with a cold butter knife so as not to heat it up too much.

Stir the lemon juice into the chilled water, then pour into the bowl, using one hand to quickly bring the dough together into a ball. Cover in plastic wrap (or eco-wrap) and chill in the fridge for at least 30 minutes.

Meanwhile, for the custard topping, put the milk, cream, and vanilla bean into a saucepan over medium heat. When the first bubbles begin to appear on the surface, immediately take off the heat, cover, and leave to infuse for about 15 minutes, then fish out the vanilla bean.

In a bowl, mix the egg yolks with the sugar and cornstarch until smooth. Pour this into the pan of vanilla-infused milk and place over low heat, stirring constantly with a wooden spoon as it thickens. If the custard seems to be thickening too quickly and is starting to look lumpy, use a whisk instead.

When you have a nice thick custard, transfer it to a cold bowl and sit that inside a bigger bowl or pan full of iced water. Stir occasionally as it cools, until it is completely cold.

Preheat the oven to 400°F (200°C) and line a baking sheet with parchment paper.

Take the dough out of the fridge and divide it in half. Return one half to the fridge and place the other half on a flour-dusted surface. Use a rolling pin to roll it out to a rectangle about ¼ inch (6 mm) thick, then cut into 2-inch (6 cm) squares and place on the baking sheet, giving them space to expand in the oven. Repeat with the other half of the dough.

Place a teaspoonful of the custard in the middle of each square and top with a few sea buckthorn berries. Sprinkle with brown sugar and bake for 15 minutes until caramelized and golden.

In the late summer, chanterelles are on every menu in the Baltics and are sold on many a street corner. This chanterelle omelet was the first meal we shared together as a family when we were reunited in Tallinn after a couple of months apart; my partner, Yasin, had been working on the other side of the world and was craving something European, seasonal and homey. If you can't find chanterelles, you could make this omelet with a mixture of other seasonal mushrooms.

CHANTERELLE OMELET

SERVES 2

- 3½ oz (100 g) chanterelle mushrooms
- 3 eggs
- 2½ tablespoons light cream
- 1½ tablespoons (25 g) butter
- 1 garlic clove, crushed
- ½ cup (50 g) grated hard cheese, such as parmesan
- 1 teaspoon Latvian green cheese (see page 245)— optional
- Salt and black pepper

VEGETARIAN

First wash the chanterelles thoroughly—I always fill a sink with cold water, put all the chanterelles in there, and then use a small knife to scrape any dirt off them. Drain the mushrooms and pat dry with paper towel, then halve or quarter any larger ones.

Crack your eggs into a bowl, add a splash of the cream, and season with salt and pepper, then beat lightly with a fork.

In a large frying pan, melt half of the butter and add the chanterelles. Fry for 7–8 minutes, stirring occasionally. Near the end of the cooking time, season well with salt and pepper, then add the garlic and remaining cream. Stir and simmer for a minute or two, then remove from the heat and set aside while you make the omelet.

Melt half of the remaining butter in a small frying pan and once it's hot, pour in half of the omelet mixture. Using a spatula, bring the set edges into the center and let the runny eggs flow into the gaps a couple of times, then just leave it to cook for about a minute.

When the omelet is almost cooked, but still a bit wet in the middle, scatter over half of the grated cheese, the green cheese (if using), and the chanterelles. Use a spatula to help fold the omelet in half and ease it out of the pan and onto a plate.

Make the other omelet in the same way, filling it with the rest of the grated cheese and chanterelles, then serve.

Poppyseeds are one of the ingredients most associated with the Baltic region. When it comes to bread products, they are often used in large quantities, as they are in these rich pastries, which are photographed on page 35. The so-called "drowned" dough for these poppyseed pastries is easier to make than your usual yeasted dough. The poppyseeds, however, need a bit of prep—ideally the evening before you want to make the pastries. Otherwise, you can buy ready-made poppyseed mix (labeled "for *Makowiec*") from any Polish food shop, or try using Plum butter (see page 189) as an alternative filling.

POPPYSEED PASTRIES

MAKES 12–16

* 1 oz (25 g) fresh yeast or ½ oz (15 g) dried yeast
* Scant ½ cup (100 ml) whole milk, warmed
* 1 tablespoon sugar
* ½ teaspoon vanilla extract
* 2 cups (250 g) all-purpose flour, plus extra for dusting
* 1 tablespoon sour cream
* 9 tablespoons (125 g) unsalted butter, softened
* Large pinch of salt
* 1 egg, lightly beaten
* Brown sugar, for sprinkling

For the filling

* ⅔ cup (100 g) poppyseeds
* 4 tablespoons honey
* 1 egg yolk
* ½ teaspoon almond extract
* Handful of raisins, soaked in ¼ cup (60 ml) rum or apple juice for about half an hour

VEGETARIAN

To prepare the poppyseeds for the filling, put them in a sieve with a very fine mesh and rinse well under running water. Tip into a heavy-based saucepan and pour in enough boiling water to cover the seeds by about a ½ inch (1 cm), then bring back to a boil and simmer for 10 minutes. Turn off the heat, cover, and leave for at least 3 hours, or preferably overnight.

In a powerful food processor at high speed, grind the poppyseeds (which will have absorbed all the liquid) until they become lighter in color and clump together, then turn the processor down a notch, add the honey, egg yolk, and almond extract, and pulse to combine. Scrape the mixture into a small bowl and stir in the drained raisins.

In a large bowl, combine the yeast with the milk and sugar, then cover with a clean tea towel and leave in a warm place for about 20 minutes or until frothy.

When the yeast mixture is bubbly, add the vanilla, flour, sour cream, butter, and salt and mix well with a wooden spoon. Once a dough starts to form, turn it out onto a flour-dusted surface and knead with your hands—it will be sticky, so gradually add more flour and keep kneading until the dough becomes manageable and comes away from your hands easily. Place the dough ball in a large saucepan full of warm water. When it rises to the top, it's ready. If it hasn't risen in 5 minutes, check to make sure it's not stuck to the bottom. Once it floats, take it out of the water and put it on a floured surface.

Preheat the oven to 350°F (180°C) and line a large baking sheet with parchment paper.

Knead the dough, adding a little flour to make it less sticky (the dough will be quite wet at this point), but not too much or the pastries will be heavy. With a rolling pin, roll out the dough into a rectangle about ½ inch (1 cm) thick, then spread with the poppyseed filling, leaving a ¾-inch (2 cm) border all around the edges. Starting from one of the longer sides, roll up the dough, tucking in the two shorter sides as you go, so you end up with a roll that is sealed at both ends.

Cut your roll into ¾-inch (2 cm) slices and place them, cut sides up, on the baking sheet, giving them room to expand in the oven. Brush with beaten egg and sprinkle with brown sugar, then bake for 25–30 minutes or until golden brown.

Kefir berry smoothie
(page 233)

Drop scones with
prunes & sour cream
(page 37)

34

*Poppyseed pastries
(page 32)*

*Kama yogurt with
plum butter
(page 36)*

The malty mixture of ground grains and peas called *kama* is one of my favorite Estonian foods, because it's so versatile—try it sprinkled over your breakfast muesli, or even as an ice-cream topping. I've discovered that you can achieve the same deliciousness without the peas and so, out of convenience, I now make my *kama* with just a mix of grains; if you would like to try the more traditional version, you can find it on page 232.

My personal preference is to use kefir yogurt in this recipe (photographed on page 35), since it's lighter than Greek-style yogurt and has more of an Eastern European tang. If you haven't made a batch of plum butter, you can simply stew some fruit over very low heat until mushy and then leave to cool slightly before using in the recipe—berries work particularly well, since they only take a few minutes.

KAMA YOGURT
WITH PLUM BUTTER

SERVES 4

* 3–4 tablespoons pumpkin seeds (pepitas)
* 3⅓ cups (800 ml) kefir yogurt or Greek-style yogurt
* 3–4 tablespoons runny honey
* 4 tablespoons Plum butter (see page 189)

For the kama

* ½ cup (50 g) rolled oats
* ½ cup (50 g) barley flakes
* ½ cup (50 g) rye flakes

VEGETARIAN

For the *kama*, place all the ingredients in a bowl, pour in enough water to cover them by about ¾ inch (2 cm), and leave to soak for 30 minutes.

Preheat the oven to 400°F (200°C).

Drain the soaked oats, barley, and rye flakes, then scatter them over a large baking sheet, spreading them out evenly. Roast for 40 minutes, stirring halfway through, then switch off the oven but leave the grains to cool in the still-warm oven. When they are ready, they should be very dry and a deep-brown color.

Tip the grains into a food processor and grind to a powder. (You could also do this in batches in a clean coffee grinder.)

Toast the pumpkin seeds in a dry frying pan over low heat for a few minutes, just until they start popping. Keep an eye on them and give them a stir occasionally so they don't burn. Remove from the heat and set aside.

In a bowl, mix together the yogurt, honey, and 8 tablespoons of the *kama* (the rest will keep for at least a month if stored in an airtight container). Place some plum butter in the bottom of each glass or bowl, top with the *kama* yogurt, and sprinkle with the toasted pumpkin seeds.

Photographed on page 34, this recipe is a Lithuanian variation on one of my favorite childhood dishes, *racuchy ze śliwkami*, or drop scones with plums. Made with dried prunes, the drop scones take on an entirely different flavor and appearance, and I can never resist serving them with grated dark chocolate—what an indulgence! If you are serving these for brunch, you can make them in advance and keep them warm in a low oven for up to an hour (don't leave them in there any longer, though, lest they dry out).

DROP SCONES
WITH PRUNES & SOUR CREAM

SERVES 2 for breakfast
or 4 as part of brunch

* 3½ oz (100 g) pitted prunes
* ⅔ cup (150 ml) boiled water, left to cool until it is just warm
* 1¼ cups (150 g) all-purpose flour
* ¼ teaspoon ground cinnamon
* Large pinch of salt
* 2 teaspoons sugar
* 1 egg
* Rapeseed oil, for frying
* Sour cream and grated dark chocolate, to serve

VEGETARIAN

First, soak the prunes in the warm water for about half an hour until soft. Drain the prunes, reserving the soaking water, then halve them.

Sift the flour into a large bowl with the cinnamon and salt. Add the sugar and crack in the egg, then slowly start adding the reserved soaking water, stirring constantly with a wooden spoon. Keep mixing until there are no lumps left, then stir in the prunes.

Preheat the oven to 200°F (100°C).

Heat 1 tablespoon of oil in a large non-stick frying pan over medium heat. Once the oil is hot, add tablespoonfuls of the batter—depending on the size of your pan, you should be able to fit three or four at a time—and cook for 3–4 minutes on each side, until golden. Drain the cooked drop scones on paper towels, then keep warm in the oven while you cook the rest, adding more oil as needed.

Serve the drop scones with sour cream and grated dark chocolate on top.

Seize truth and strength, oh shades of old!
Show lost faces of our forebears,
The brave exploits of man and magician
The coursings of the great Kalevs!

FROM *KALEVIPOEG* ("*THE SON OF KALEV*"),
BY FRIEDRICH REINHOLD KREUTZWALD

TALLINN:

FROM MEDIEVAL CITY TO HIGH-TECH HUB

My daughter Nusia and I flew into Tallinn, the capital of Estonia, over Lake Ülemiste— a lake said to be formed from the tears shed by Kalev's widow, Linda. According to Estonia's national epic, their youngest son, born after Kalev's death, became the heroic Kalevipoeg ("son of Kalev"). While fighting for his country and its people, Kalevipoeg also made very human mistakes during his many adventures, which have been recounted through the ages but were only written down, in verse form, in the mid-nineteenth century.

Landing at what appeared to be a miniature airport dotted with tiny book-lending libraries, I immediately warmed to Estonia, which seemed friendly and perhaps even a little bit magical. There was no chance for us to settle down with a book, though. Within twenty minutes of landing, we were in a taxi driven by a smiley gold-toothed driver who was keen to try out his Polish, and ready to whisk us to where we were staying.

By the time we had arrived at our accommodation near the Old Town, the slowly setting summer sun was bathing everything in molten gold, so we went for a walk to make the most of the glorious light. We wandered the streets, fueled by Estonian-style hotdogs with beets, pickles, dill, and garlicky sour cream that I remember as being called "welcome to Tallinn." Perhaps that was wishful thinking— but as Nusia fed her leftover bun to the tiny, enterprising birds, I certainly felt welcomed, the relaxed atmosphere of this amicable city balm for a frazzled traveler.

At a nearby play area, we fell into conversation with Maria, who was visiting from Saint Petersburg. Having grown up in Tallinn and studied in Poland, she too was keen to practice her Polish, and as we talked she foisted handfuls of berries on us from a massive plastic bucket at her feet.

We feasted on ripe gooseberries, tart redcurrants, and exploding pink raspberries, all picked from her father's garden, before wending our way back to the apartment, tired but excited. My partner, Yasin, was flying in to join us later that evening, and our family Baltic adventure was about to begin.

I was charmed by Tallinn's relaxed atmosphere, delicious produce, and the marzipan-colored buildings of its UNESCO World Heritage-listed Old Town.

41

The next day we went to the Balti Jaam artisanal market to stock up, returning with bags full of enticing produce: chanterelles, which we fried in butter and tucked inside fluffy omelets; malty black bread, to be spread with various fish roes; juicy heirloom tomatoes that needed no dressing; and plump berries, to be eaten with dollops of locally made yogurt. Everything was piled onto the disproportionately small kitchen table, and we washed down our Estonian banquet with refreshing *kvass*, a fermented drink made with bread. In the afternoon, we explored the extensive and well-preserved Old Town, walking through a gateway, past statues of looming faceless monks, down a thousand steps, and entering a maze of cobbled streets and marzipan-like houses.

✖

Although there had been a settlement in Tallinn since 3000 BC, it went by many other names—"Lindanäs" in Swedish, "Kolyvan" in Russian, and "Reval" in German, along with variations of all three—betraying its complicated history. We do know that there was a culture here in the first century BC, as recorded by Roman chronicler Tacitus. From this place, which he named Aesti, ancient Estonians exported amber and traded with the Vikings.

The Germans arrived in the thirteenth century, with the Teutonic Knights ruling the southern part of the territory, while the Danes established themselves in the north. When the Danes took control of the fortifications on Toompea, the city's landmark hill, the name Tallinn ("Danish castle") was born.

Estonians were pagan until their forced conversion by the Teutonic Knights, and it seems that such long-held beliefs remain deeply rooted in the culture. Apparently, 69 percent of Estonians today believe that trees have souls, and only 14 percent say they follow a religion. So when one of the world's first Christmas trees (Riga also stakes a claim in this respect) was erected in the main square of Tallinn in 1441, I imagine much of the celebration honored the tree itself, rather than the Christian traditions of the Germanic ruling classes. Nevertheless, there was dancing, drinking, and singing around the tree, which was then ceremonially burned.

Over the years, Sweden, Russia, Denmark, and Poland have all sought to control Tallinn. The Swedes initially triumphed over Russia in the sixteenth century, bringing a period of prosperity. However, after the Great Northern War, Russia took control again, although the Germanic influence remained strong. There was a brief lull for the city ahead of World War II and Nazi occupation, followed by the Soviets, who stayed for nearly fifty years.

While calling Tallinn lucky would be specious, it is at least lucky enough not to have suffered wartime destruction. The Old Town's stunning medieval buildings have withstood the test of both time and invasions, with two kilometers of the walls remaining intact and twenty-six of the original forty-six towers still standing. And the Orthodox crosses atop the onion domes of Alexander Nevsky Cathedral still gleam in the sunlight. Although the past surrounds you here, this is not a backward-looking city, but rather somewhere the past and future seem to happily co-exist, and it clearly has a special pull for many creatives.

Even in the remotest neck of the woods in Estonia, you are connected to high-speed internet, and technological research has been liberalized, encouraging innovation. These factors are big draws for start-up companies, and I wasn't surprised to learn that the Skype software was developed by Estonians.

The progressive and enterprising nature of the Estonian people is also reflected in their cuisine. Tallinn is where I sampled ice-cream flavors including sprat (not a fan) and black charcoal with white chocolate (a definite favorite). Here, local produce and traditions from years past are amalgamated, creating something new each day. This fresh energy makes Tallinn an exciting place to be right now and a place to watch in the future.

✖

Sunrise over the medieval towers of Tallinn's city walls.

APPETIZERS & SNACKS

Traditionally, the Baltic States have subscribed wholeheartedly to the Eastern European way of doing appetizers. This means greeting guests with an abundant table, overflowing with colorful plates bearing artfully arranged salads, cheeses, cold cuts, ferments, bread, and butter.

Yet when eating in a modern Baltic restaurant, we were served appetizers in the way we are accustomed to in the West—as a little something to whet our appetite before the main course. The recipes in this chapter have been chosen to give you the best of both worlds.

Wreaths feature in the folklore of the Baltics and beyond, so when I came across a wreath of appetizers in a cutting-edge Lithuanian restaurant it struck a deep emotional chord. I decided there and then that this was the perfect symbol of Baltic cuisine: modern and unique, yet deeply rooted in tradition. On my return home, I designed my own Baltic wreath to serve at my supper clubs, based around a braid of dark rye bread—there's nothing like breaking bread across a table to bring people together. And if there's any left after the first course, it can then be used to dip into a second course of soup.

Rye has long been favored in the Baltics, since it's a hardy crop that can survive the cold. While wholewheat flour is usually my preference, for this wreath I use a combination of light rye and white bread flour to create the perfect crunch. Red rye malt powder adds depth of flavor, but feel free to use cacao powder instead or skip it altogether. As is usual with yeasty things, the wreath tastes best on the day it's made—ideally while it's still warm.

On top, you might have wild mushroom terrine with fermented berries, smoked fish, and fermented vegetables, all interwoven with pea shoots and colorful flowers. Local is always best when it comes to edible blooms—I like to use hawthorn when it's in season, as you can eat both the leaves and white blossom (and they say it's good for your heart). You can play with the toppings as much as you like; the important thing is to make it feel celebratory. Here are some of my favorites to get you started.

A BALTIC WREATH

SERVES 4

* 1½ cups (150 g) light rye flour
* 1 cup (150 g) white bread flour, plus extra for dusting
* 1 heaped teaspoon salt
* 1 teaspoon instant yeast
* 1 tablespoon red rye malt powder (see page 246) or cacao powder
* 1 teaspoon molasses, mixed with a generous ¾ cup (200 ml) warm water

Combine the flours in a large mixing bowl, then add the salt, yeast, and rye malt powder or cacao powder. Mix well, then pour in the molasses water and, using one hand, bring everything together into a dough. Turn out onto a lightly floured work surface and knead for 5 minutes or until smooth and elastic.

Return the dough to the bowl, cover with a clean tea towel, and leave in a warm place for 5 hours to proof. At least three times during the proofing process, punch down the dough and fold it over, repeating this action about five or six times.

Suggested toppings

* Wild mushroom & pumpkin terrine (see page 54)
* Juniper-smoked herring (see page 56)
* Easy home-cured ham (see page 187)
* Smoked salmon
* Caviar or salmon roe
* Medium- or hard-boiled quail's eggs
* Fermented red cabbage (see page 176)
* Fermented gooseberries or cranberries (see page 182)
* Fermented celery & carrot (see page 183)
* Beaten-up cucumbers (see page 188)
* Pea shoots
* Chive flowers
* Three-cornered leeks with flowers
* Hawthorn leaves and blossom
* Jack-by-the-hedge flowers

Towards the end of the proofing time, preheat the oven to 400°F (200°C) and lightly flour a large sheet of parchment paper or a baking sheet.

Place the proofed dough on the parchment paper or baking sheet and, using your hands, make a hole in the middle and pull the dough outwards into an even circle shape. With kitchen scissors, make incisions in the circle at 2-inch (5 cm) intervals, then pull the edges apart to create the effect of leaves.

Bake for 20–25 minutes or until it sounds hollow when tapped underneath.

Transfer the wreath to a serving platter and arrange your chosen toppings around it, then place in the center of the table and let people help themselves.

A Baltic wreath (page 50)

Wild mushroom &
pumpkin terrine
(page 54)

Easy home-cured
ham (page 187)

While I love eating any kind of pâté or terrine—and ate plenty of them in the Baltics—I don't love making meaty pâté. All that squishing of ground meat puts me off. Wild mushrooms, on the other hand, are an absolute pleasure to work with. At home you will often find me with my nose in a large tub of dried wild mushrooms; their visceral smell takes me deep into the stillness of a dark wood, where all is as it should be. If you are Eastern European, you will probably be accustomed to getting your stash of dried wild mushrooms from family members who went picking at the tail end of summer and then lovingly cleaned and dried their harvest in the last of the year's sunshine. Otherwise, you should be able to find them in any Polish or Italian deli. I find that this earthy terrine (photographed on page 53) tastes even better with tart little bombs of fermented gooseberry or cranberry (see page 182).

If you want to make this recipe vegan, replace the egg with the following: 3 tablespoons of ground flaxseed mixed with 6 tablespoons of water in a small bowl, left to stand for about 5 minutes—this works as an egg substitute to bind the terrine. I've made it with neither egg nor soaked flaxseed before too and although it turned out great, the consistency was softer and it did fall apart more easily.

WILD MUSHROOM & PUMPKIN TERRINE

MAKES enough to fill
a 1 lb (450 g) loaf pan.

* 3½ oz (100 g) dried wild
  mushrooms
* Kettle of boiled water
* 1 medium parsnip, peeled
  and cut into chunks
* 1 medium carrot, peeled
  and cut into chunks
* ¼ celeriac, peeled and
  cut into chunks
* 2 slices peeled pumpkin
  or butternut squash,
  each about 6 inches x
  1½ inches (15 cm x 4 cm)
* 7 oz (200 g) fresh mixed
  mushrooms, coarsely chopped
* Rapeseed oil, for frying
* ½ teaspoon garlic powder
* 1 red onion (or 2 French
  shallots), finely chopped
* 1¼ cups (150 g) walnut pieces
* 1¾ oz (50 g) pumpkin seeds
  (pepitas)
* 1 tablespoon dried
  breadcrumbs
* 1 egg, lightly beaten, or
  3 tablespoons soaked
  flaxseed—see opposite
* 1 garlic clove, crushed to
  a paste with a pinch of salt,
  using the flat of a knife
  (or 1 heaped teaspoon
  garlic paste)
* Handful of dried cranberries
* Handful of finely chopped
  flat-leaf parsley
* Salt and black pepper

VEGETARIAN/
VEGAN

Some store-bought dried wild mushrooms are already cleaned, so check the instructions on the package. Otherwise, it's worth giving your dried mushrooms a thorough cleaning to avoid ending up with a gritty terrine!

First, put the mushrooms in a sieve and rinse under cold running water. Pour hot water from the kettle over them to open their cups and then rinse them under the cold tap again, rubbing them gently with your fingers. Tip the mushrooms into a heatproof bowl, cover with more hot water from the kettle, and leave to stand for 20 minutes, then drain and return to the rinsed-out bowl. Finally, pour in enough hot water from the kettle to cover the mushrooms by 2 inches (5 cm)—about 1¼ cups (300 ml)—then cover and allow to soak for at least 4 hours or overnight.

Transfer the wild mushrooms and their soaking liquid into a small saucepan and simmer for 30 minutes or until tender, then drain.

Meanwhile, cook the parsnip, carrot, and celeriac in boiling salted water until soft, then drain and mash until smooth. Set aside.

Parboil the pumpkin or squash slices in boiling salted water for about 5 minutes—they should still be firm. Drain and pat dry with paper towels.

Working in batches, fry the fresh mushrooms in a large frying pan over medium heat, using a tablespoon of oil at a time, until golden brown, then season each batch with salt, pepper, and a sprinkling of garlic powder. When all the mushrooms are done, leave them to cool slightly.

In the same pan, fry the onion in another tablespoon of oil until soft and browned, then set aside to cool.

Lightly toast the walnuts and pumpkin seeds in a dry frying pan over medium heat, then tip out onto a plate and leave to cool.

Preheat the oven to 350°F (180°C). Grease a 1 lb (450 g) loaf pan and dust with the breadcrumbs.

Put the cooled fried mushrooms into a food processor with the wild mushrooms, onion, walnuts, and pumpkin seeds. Grind everything together to a rough paste, then add to the mashed root vegetables. Finally, add the egg or soaked flaxseed, garlic paste, cranberries, and parsley. Season generously with salt and pepper and use your hands to combine thoroughly.

Scrape about a third of the terrine mixture into the loaf pan, pressing it down firmly, then place a slice of pumpkin on top. Add another third of the terrine mixture on top, followed by the other slice of pumpkin, and then the rest of the terrine mixture. Press each layer down well, so that the terrine is tightly packed. Bake for 30 minutes or until browned and crisp on top. Switch off the oven and allow the terrine to cool in the oven (I usually leave it overnight).

To serve, carefully turn out the terrine and cut into slices.

DIY is not my strong point, so if I can build a mini-smoker, anyone can! All you need is an old cookie tin, a small metal rack that will fit inside the tin, some foil, and wood chips. (I like to use birch-wood chips because my Grandma Halinka instilled in me a love of the birch tree, which is considered to have "good energy" in Lithuania, where she grew up.) Line the cookie tin with foil—this makes it easier to clean afterwards—then scatter a large handful of wood chips in the bottom and sit your metal rack over them. Make sure you can close the tin and you are ready to go.

Another option is to use a large pot with a tight-fitting lid and a colander that fits comfortably inside it. Line the pot with foil to protect it, then place a handful of wood chips in the bottom and sit the colander on top. Line the top edge of the colander with foil too, so the smoke cannot escape. Lay the fish in the colander, then cover the pot tightly with foil and the lid.

Once your smoker is smoking, it's safest to take it outdoors—into the garden or onto a balcony, if you have one, or next to an open window. Fish you smoke yourself tastes entirely different to the store-bought stuff, and this juniper-smoked herring tastes fantastic with homemade mayonnaise (see page 58, but leave out the chives) and a sprinkling of chopped dill.

JUNIPER-SMOKED HERRING

SERVES 4 as part of a platter or 2 as a main dish

- ✳ 3½ oz (100 g) wood chips
- ✳ 1 tablespoon juniper berries, lightly crushed
- ✳ 2 herring fillets
- ✳ Salt and black pepper

PESCATARIAN

Prepare your smoker in one of the ways described above, laying a bed of the wood chips and juniper berries in the base. Season the herring fillets with salt and pepper.

Place your smoker over medium-high heat until the wood chips start smoking, then remove from the heat and smoke your herrings for at least 10 minutes; I like to wait until the wood chips stop smoking completely for a stronger flavor.

You can eat these smoked herrings either warm or cold. They will keep in the fridge for up to 3 days and you can then reheat them in the oven or give them a quick blast under the broiler.

Just as the Siberian Yupik have many words for snow, Eastern Europeans have many words for fried little round things. This recipe was inspired by a vegetarian cookbook dating from 1929 that was printed in Lithuania, but (luckily for me) written in Polish, and with an entire chapter devoted to vegetable patties. These earthy chestnut ones work incredibly well with something crunchy and fresh on the side—perhaps one of the slaws on pages 148–151 or just some peppery salad greens with a zesty vinaigrette.

OLD-STYLE CHESTNUT PATTIES

SERVES 4 as an appetizer

* 1 white bread bun, ideally stale
* Generous ¾ cup (200 ml) whole milk
* 30 cooked and peeled chestnuts—about 6½ oz (180 g)
* 1 small onion
* 1 egg, lightly beaten
* Handful of finely chopped flat-leaf parsley
* ¼ teaspoon freshly grated nutmeg
* 1 cup (100 g) dried breadcrumbs, for coating
* Rapeseed oil, for frying
* Salt and white pepper

VEGETARIAN

In a saucepan, soak the bread in the milk for 30 minutes, pushing it under the surface and giving it a squeeze halfway through.

Process the chestnuts and onion in a food processor until coarsely chopped (or you can grate them). Add the chestnuts and onion to the pan. Bring to a boil, then turn the heat right down and simmer, stirring constantly, for 2–3 minutes, until you have a thick batter. Remove from the heat and allow to cool slightly before mixing in the egg, parsley, and nutmeg. Season well with salt and pepper.

Scatter the breadcrumbs over a tray or large plate. Take tablespoonfuls of the mixture and use wet hands to form into balls—they will be sticky, so roll them in the breadcrumbs as you shape them, then gently flatten each one.

Preheat the oven to 200°F (100°C). Pour a film of rapeseed oil into a large frying pan and place over medium heat. Working in batches, fry the patties for 2 minutes on each side, or until golden brown, then drain on paper towels. Keep warm in the oven while you cook the rest, then serve immediately.

We were at a beach shack in the Latvian seaside resort of Liepāja, on the edge of a vast expanse of powdery sand. Well, more like a concrete box, really, but it was perfectly placed for selling fried fish and seafood to hungry beach-goers. Every afternoon of our stay we sat here, our metal tables and chairs warmed by the glow of the setting sun, eating salty fried sprats out of paper cones.

If the fishmonger hasn't already cleaned the sprats for you, start to cut across just below the head, pulling out the guts just before you cut right through, then rinse out the cavity and pat dry. If you can't get sprats you could use other small fish such as whitebait—in which case, there's no need to remove the heads or guts.

SEMOLINA-FRIED SPRATS
WITH CHIVE MAYONNAISE

SERVES 4 as a snack

* 3 tablespoons semolina flour
* 3 tablespoons all-purpose flour
* 1 tablespoon "herbs for fish" (see page 136)
* 12 sprats, cleaned and heads removed (or other small fish like whitebait)
* 4¼ cups (1 liter) rapeseed oil, for deep-frying
* Salt flakes and lemon wedges, to serve

For the chive mayonnaise

* 2 egg yolks
* ⅔ cup (150 ml) cold-pressed rapeseed oil
* 2 teaspoons lemon juice
* 1 tablespoon chopped chives
* Salt and white pepper

PESCATARIAN

First make your chive mayonnaise. Place the egg yolks in a large bowl and season with salt and pepper. Now, whisking constantly, add a small drop of oil, then another, and continue, a drop at a time, until the yolks and oil emulsify and start to thicken. At this point, you can slowly start to add more oil, eventually creating a steady, slow stream. Once all the oil has been incorporated, whisk in the lemon juice and chives, then adjust the seasoning to taste. Chill in the fridge until ready to serve.

Mix together the two flours and the "herbs for fish," then divide between two large plates. Place six sprats on each plate and dust liberally with the flour mixture.

Heat the deep-frying oil in a medium-sized, heavy-based pot. Once the oil is hot and little bubbles have started to appear, fry the sprats four at a time for about 5 minutes, stirring so they cook evenly, until crisp and golden brown.

Drain on paper towels, then sprinkle with salt flakes and squeeze over some lemon juice. Serve with the chive mayonnaise.

On a rainy day in Riga, I met food expert Linda in a slick, modern restaurant. I had so many questions about Latvian food, and Linda had all the answers. As we parted, she invited me to dinner at her friend Madara's house the following evening. On arrival, I was greeted with sparkling wine and this flavorful tomato tart that I just couldn't get enough of. When I asked Linda the secret, she said, "really good butter." Her flaky pastry really is wonderful, and I'm sure she'd be horrified to learn that I sometimes use pre-made puff pastry when I'm in a hurry ... However, when I do make my own, I tend to do it the day before making the tart, leaving the pastry parcel in the fridge overnight and rolling it out the following day, which simplifies the process!

Great tomatoes are essential for this. Linda used colorful heirloom tomatoes, which are ideal in summer. In wintertime, I use the ripest, most flavorful tomatoes I can find. Which brings us to the special ingredient that elevates this dish to something truly incredible, *zaļais siers* ("green cheese"). Available direct from the producer in Latvia (see page 245), this grated dried curd cheese is colored and flavored with blue fenugreek, and it brings a pungent, umami note to many foods—including pasta and soups—so it won't go to waste. Otherwise, for a similar flavor, try combining finely grated parmesan or pecorino with ground blue fenugreek (see page 245 for suggested proportions).

LINDA'S TOMATO TART
WITH LATVIAN GREEN CHEESE

SERVES 4–6

* 1 egg, lightly beaten
* 4 large, ripe tomatoes
* 2 tablespoons grated Latvian green cheese
* Salt flakes and black pepper

For the puff pastry

* 2 cups (250 g) all-purpose flour, plus extra for dusting
* ¼ teaspoon salt
* ⅔ cup (150 ml) chilled water
* 2 sticks (225 g) cold unsalted butter, diced
* 1 egg, lightly beaten

VEGETARIAN

For the puff pastry, place the flour and salt in a food processor and start to pulse while you pour in the chilled water. As soon as it forms a rough dough, remove from the processor and knead very briefly, just to shape the dough into a ball. Alternatively, you can bring the dough together by hand, using a knife or fork to help bring it together at first, then briefly kneading and shaping the dough into a ball. Wrap in plastic wrap (or eco-wrap) and chill in the fridge for at least 30 minutes.

Lightly sprinkle the butter with flour, then place it between two sheets of parchment paper and bash it all over with a rolling pin to soften it. Remove the top sheet of parchment paper, cut the butter in half, and place one half on top of the other, then sprinkle it with a little more flour and use your rolling pin to reshape it into a rectangle about 6 inches x 4 inches (15 cm x 10 cm).

Take the dough out of the fridge and, on a flour-dusted work surface, roll it out into a rough 10-inch (25 cm) square. Place the butter in the center and fold over the right and left sides of the pastry so that they overlap in the middle, then fold in the top and bottom, pressing out any trapped air bubbles. Roll out the pastry to make a rectangle about 12 inches x 6 inches (30 cm x 15 cm). Now mentally mark it into thirds and make a parcel by folding down the top to cover the middle third, and then the bottom up to overlap. Rotate the dough one-quarter turn and roll out into the same-sized rectangle again, then repeat the parcel-making process, folding down from the top and up from the bottom. Lightly dust the pastry with flour as you go, so it doesn't stick. Rotate the pastry another quarter-turn and repeat, then re-wrap and chill in the fridge for at least 20 minutes, or overnight.

Repeat the whole parcel-making process two more times, then chill the pastry for a final hour before using.

Preheat the oven to 400°F (200°C). Lightly grease a baking sheet.

Cut the tomatoes into ¼-inch (6 mm) slices, then gently pat dry with paper towels.

On a flour-dusted work surface, roll out your chilled pastry to a rectangle about ⅛-inch (3 mm) thick. Place on the baking sheet, then create a border all the way around by lightly running a knife ¾ inch (2 cm) from the edge. Glaze the border with the beaten egg, then arrange the tomato slices inside it in a single layer. Sprinkle with the grated cheese, salt flakes, and a few grinds of pepper, then bake until the pastry border is golden brown, puffed, and crisp, 20–25 minutes.

Let the tart cool for 10 minutes before cutting into slices to serve.

Fishing is a national pastime throughout the Baltics, with various fish festivals held across the region. Greta, a Lithuanian foodie friend I met through Instagram who lives in London, told me about a festival she remembered from her childhood in Klaipėda that celebrated "little fish that taste like cucumber when they're cooked."

Frozen fish is said to have originated in the north of Russia and I would go as far as to call it the Eastern European sashimi—and, as with sashimi, you must of course use the freshest, best-quality raw fish you can find. Once you have sourced the primary ingredient, this is an extraordinarily simple dish to make. I like to use halibut, but it's best to go with whatever white fish your fishmonger recommends for sashimi on the day.

Frozen fish is usually eaten with spicy condiments such as radish and onion, or pungent horseradish sauce, however I have been known to eat the fish curls (which you inevitably get when the frozen fish is sliced very thinly) simply with salt flakes. I just love the sensation of the curl melting and unfolding on my tongue, as well as its umami flavor.

FROZEN FISH
WITH QUICK-PICKLED RADISHES

SERVES 4 as an appetizer

* 7 oz (200 g) sashimi-quality halibut or other white fish, filleted
* 1 red onion, thinly sliced
* Juice of ½ lemon
* Crushed ice, to serve
* Sprinkling of finely chopped chives
* Salt flakes

For the radishes

* 2 cups (500 ml) cider vinegar
* ⅓ cup (70 g) sugar
* 1 bay leaf
* 5 black peppercorns
* 3½ oz (100 g) radishes, thinly sliced

PESCATARIAN

As soon as you arrive home with your fish, place it in the freezer and leave it there for an hour or until it is frozen solid.

Meanwhile, make the quick-pickled radishes. In a stainless steel saucepan, combine the vinegar with the sugar, bay leaf, and peppercorns. Bring to a boil and simmer until the sugar has completely dissolved, then set aside to cool completely. Place your radishes in the cooled brine and chill in the fridge for at least 20 minutes.

In a small bowl, steep the onion in the lemon juice for 20 minutes.

Remove the radishes from the brine and the onion from the lemon juice, then place them on a plate with some crushed ice on it. Sprinkle the chives over the radishes and onion.

Take out your frozen fish and slice it thinly with a vegetable peeler, cheese slicer, or very sharp knife. Only slice what you will eat right away, since the fish must not defrost.

Arrange the fish slices next to the radishes, onions, and chives on the ice. Sprinkle with salt flakes, then serve immediately.

To make this quintessential Baltic loaf, you'll need to get your sourdough starter under way three days beforehand (unless you already have one going, of course). I used to make mine from just rye flour and water, but in the Baltics I learned to use something that has live cultures in it, like kefir or buttermilk. This makes perfect sense and works brilliantly—after only a day my starter was bubbling away, so make sure you use a large jar!

If you intend to make bread regularly, leave about a quarter of the starter in the jar and add ¾ cup (100 g) rye flour, along with enough tepid water—boiled and left to cool—to bring it back to much the same consistency it was before. You can then keep it in the fridge, but it needs to be fed. Ideally, you'd make bread every five days or so, taking your starter out 24 hours in advance and waking it up by feeding it with a couple of tablespoons of rye flour and about the same amount of tepid water. If you leave your starter for longer than a week in the fridge untended, it may die, although I have been known to neglect mine for two weeks and still managed to bring it back to life …

You can buy oat bran or flax bran from health food stores and red rye malt powder from specialist baking suppliers (see page 246).

BLACK BREAD

MAKES 1 loaf

* ⅓ cup (80 ml) molasses
* 1 tablespoon unsalted butter, plus extra for greasing
* 4 cups (500 g) wholemeal rye flour, plus extra for dusting
* 1 tablespoon salt
* 2 tablespoons red rye malt powder—optional
* 3 tablespoons oat and/or flax bran
* 1¼ cups (300 ml) tepid water
* Caraway seeds, for sprinkling

For the sourdough starter

* 1½ cups (200 g) whole-grain rye flour
* 1¼ cups (300 ml) milk kefir
* ½ teaspoon sugar

For the sourdough starter, mix all the ingredients together in a large jar. Cover the jar with cheesecloth or a clean tea towel and leave at room temperature for 3–4 days (the starter should be bubbly and lively-looking by then), giving it a stir each day.

When you are ready to make the bread, put the molasses and butter into a small saucepan and heat, stirring regularly, for a couple of minutes, just until the butter has melted and the mixture is runny. Set aside to cool until it is just warm.

Put all the dry ingredients into a large bowl, add the tepid water and three-quarters of your starter culture, and mix well with a wooden spoon. Add the molasses mixture and mix to a rough dough. Turn out onto a flour-dusted work surface and knead for a few minutes, incorporating more flour as needed, just until it comes together into a ball. (Black bread doesn't need anywhere near as much kneading as white bread—in fact, some people don't knead it at all.) Lightly grease a 2 lb (900 g) loaf pan. Place the dough in the pan, cover with a clean tea towel, and leave in a warm place (next to a radiator, for example) for 10–12 hours—it won't double in size but should grow considerably.

Preheat the oven to 350°F (180°C), then half-fill a roasting pan with water and place it in the bottom of the oven. Sprinkle your loaf with caraway seeds and slide it onto the middle shelf. Bake for 1 hour or until it sounds hollow when tapped on the base. Allow to cool before slicing. This bread is great with home-cured ham (see page 187) and pickles (see page 188).

RYE OPEN SANDWICHES

Open sandwiches are as popular in the Baltics as they are in neighboring Scandinavia and Poland. They may be served as a casual meal in themselves or as part of a larger table of appetizers and snacks. The art of making open sandwiches lies in creating the perfect balance of flavors and textures, as well as an aesthetically pleasing appearance. Start with Black bread (see page 64) and add your chosen toppings: here are some of my favorites.

EGG, SALAD & CAVIAR

* Butter
* Salad greens
* Heirloom tomatoes, sliced
* Hard-boiled eggs, sliced
* Caviar or other fish roe
* Salt

PESCATARIAN

A classic combination. Most Eastern European countries have their own local caviars, which I always love to try. With so many kinds of fish roe available, there's no need to go for the really expensive stuff.

This topping is fairly self-explanatory: butter the bread, then top with salad greens, tomatoes (salt), and egg (more salt) and a teaspoon of caviar. Inevitably it all falls apart as it reaches your mouth ...

HERBY CURD & CHARRED FENNEL

* Fennel, quartered lengthways
* Rapeseed oil, for drizzling
* *Twaróg* or farmer cheese
* Sour cream
* Chopped dill and mint
* Salt and white pepper
* Fermented gooseberries (see page 182), to serve—optional

VEGETARIAN

A flavorful vegetarian option (photographed on page 68), this makes a wonderful, light meal in itself—I find two slices perfect for lunch.

Drizzle the fennel with rapeseed oil, season with salt and pepper, and stick under the broiler for about 4 minutes, turning halfway through, until it has softened and is slightly charred.

In the meantime, mash the cheese to a smooth-ish consistency with a little sour cream. Add the herbs and season well with salt and pepper.

Spread the curd cheese on the bread, then top with the charred fennel and a few fermented gooseberries, if using.

HERRING SALAD

SERVES 4

* 8 oz (225 g) salted herring fillets in oil, drained
* ½ red bell pepper, finely diced
* ½ orange or yellow bell pepper, finely diced
* Generous ¾ cup (200 g) sour cream
* 2 tablespoons mayonnaise
* 2 pickles in brine, drained and diced
* ½ red onion, finely chopped
* Handful of chopped dill

PESCATARIAN

Venturing into the Estonian countryside from Tallinn, I was anticipating a fairly uneventful time, but the first place I visited was a village gallery housed in a farmhouse, complete with chickens and sheep. There, in the final rays of the setting sun, a young girl and her mother singing local folk music brought me to tears, and I ate herring salad on dark rye, washed down with blackberry wine. Here's my version, to be eaten with rye bread or fried potatoes. By far the best herring to use for this are fillets *a'la matjas*, sold in Polish shops and some supermarkets—they are not cooked but salted, soaked, and preserved in oil.

Chop the herrings and place in a large bowl. Add all the other ingredients, reserving a little of the dill to garnish, then mix well.

WILD GARLIC HUMMUS & FERMENTED GARLIC SCAPES

SERVES 4

* 3½ oz (100 g) wild garlic leaves (ramsons)
* ½ cup (100 g) dried chickpeas, cooked, or 1 x 14 oz (400 g) can of chickpeas
* Scant ½ cup (100 ml) cold-pressed rapeseed oil
* Juice of 1 lemon
* 8 Fermented garlic scapes (see page 179)
* Salt and black pepper

VEGETARIAN/
VEGAN

I tried wild garlic hummus (photographed on page 68) for the first time in Estonia, bought from an ordinary supermarket, and I was hooked! The quantity of wild garlic below makes quite a strongly flavored hummus, so if you would prefer it milder, just use half the amount. And if you happen to have a jar of Fermented wild garlic (see page 178) in your pantry, feel free to use that instead—in which case, there's no wilting required, just drain it well.

Blanch the wild garlic in a saucepan of simmering water for a minute or so, just until wilted. Drain well, then place in a food processor.

Drain the chickpeas, reserving the liquid (aquafaba) if you want to use it in vegan recipes—it will keep in the fridge for up to a week. Add the chickpeas to the food processor and process to a puree, drizzling in the oil in a steady stream, followed by the lemon juice.

Season really well with salt and pepper, then serve on rye bread with fermented garlic scapes on top.

*Wild garlic hummus
(page 67)*

*Rye open sandwich with
herby curd & charred
fennel (page 66)*

*Crescent-moon
pastries with herby
cheese filling
(page 70)*

Chive mayonnaise
(page 58)

Rye open sandwich with wild
garlic hummus & fermented
garlic scapes (page 67)

At a bakery by a gleaming river on the border of the Gauja national park, these *radziņš* —crescent-moon-shaped pastries filled with savory cheese or spiced meat and topped with crunchy seeds—were the first snack I came across in Latvia. They reminded me of the sweet, yeasty *rogaliki* (also known as *rugelach*) I remember from my childhood in Poland, but because of their salty filling, they are perhaps better suited to a beer snack than breakfast. These savory pastries are photographed on page 69; when we were shooting them, we also made the happy discovery that they taste great dipped into the chive mayo on page 58.

CRESCENT-MOON PASTRIES
WITH HERBY CHEESE FILLING

MAKES about 20

* 1 oz (25 g) fresh yeast or ½ oz (15 g) dried yeast
* Scant ½ cup (100 ml) warm whole milk
* ½ teaspoon sugar
* 2 cups (250 g) all-purpose flour, plus extra for dusting
* 1 tablespoon sour cream
* 9 tablespoons (125 g) unsalted butter, softened
* Pinch of salt
* 1 egg yolk, for glazing
* Sesame seeds and pumpkin seeds (pepitas), for sprinkling

For the filling

* 9 oz (250 g) *twaróg* or farmer cheese
* 2 tablespoons chopped dill
* 2 tablespoons chopped chives
* 2 tablespoons sour cream
* Salt and white pepper

VEGETARIAN

In a large bowl, combine the yeast with the milk and sugar, then cover with a clean tea towel and leave in a warm place for 20 minutes or until frothy.

For the filling, place all the ingredients in another bowl, season with salt and pepper, and mash together with a fork.

When the yeast mixture is bubbly, add the flour, sour cream, butter, and salt and mix well with a wooden spoon. Once a dough starts to form, turn it out onto a flour-dusted surface and knead with your hands—it will be sticky, so gradually add more flour and keep kneading until the dough becomes manageable and comes away from your hands easily. Place the dough ball in a large pot full of warm water. When it rises to the top it's ready. If it hasn't risen in 5 minutes, check to make sure it's not stuck to the bottom. Once it floats, take it out of the water and put it on a floured surface.

Meanwhile, preheat the oven to 350°F (180°C) and line a large baking sheet with parchment paper.

Knead the dough again, dusting with more flour as needed, until it is smooth and elastic. Clean your work surface, dust once more with flour, then roll out the dough to a thickness of 1/16 inch (1–2 mm). Cut into rectangles about 6 inches x 4 inches (15 cm x 10 cm), then cut each rectangle in half on the diagonal to make two triangles.

Place a teaspoon of filling on the shorter side of the triangle, then roll up towards the pointy end. Place on the baking sheet and pull the ends downwards to make a crescent-moon shape. Continue with the remaining dough and filling.

Brush your crescent moons with egg yolk, sprinkle with the seeds, and bake for 25 minutes or until golden.

If you have made some sourdough starter, but haven't baked bread for a while and it's sitting aimlessly in your fridge, you could try to wake it up and activate it, or you could just make these tasty pancake bites. You want to make sure your starter is the correct consistency first—it should be like very thick cream. If it's too thick, just mix some tepid water into it about an hour before you start the recipe.

SOURDOUGH PANCAKE BITES

SERVES 4

* ½ cup (100 g) inactive sourdough starter (see page 64)
* 2 tablespoons all-purpose flour
* 1 tablespoon rapeseed oil
* 1 tablespoon Latvian green cheese (see page 245) or 2 tablespoons grated hard cheese, such as pecorino or parmesan
* Sour cream, chopped chives, and salt, to serve

VEGETARIAN

Place the starter in a bowl with the flour and mix until you have a smooth batter.

Put the rapeseed oil in a frying pan over medium heat. When the oil is hot, pour in the batter and fry for 3–4 minutes until golden brown.

Carefully flip the pancake, sprinkle the cheese on top, and cook for another 3–4 minutes. Drain on paper towels.

Cut the pancake into triangles and serve with chive-spiked sour cream, seasoned with salt, for dipping.

Bruin the bear, who breaks free from the shackles of slavery, can be seen as a symbol of the Estonian spirit. Sadly, though, the bear's story does not end well—he is destroyed by his own kind, out of jealousy. Still, his escape represents a brave bid for freedom, and Masing, the early-nineteenth-century author of the poem "Bruin," was a great advocate for the Estonian language, with an egalitarian attitude to literature that was unusual in his time.

This "cake" may seem unusual, but I was assured that Estonians love to dig into a sandwich cake at a party, and on trying it, I must concede that it works incredibly well in between swigs of beer. The choice of fillings is limited by your imagination alone, and I have seen people getting very creative with their sandwich cakes. I, on the other hand, like to keep things simple, in sandwich cakes as in life, and my fondness for British-style cucumber sandwiches leads to me suggest using soft white sliced bread in this recipe.

ESTONIAN SANDWICH "CAKE" FOR A PARTY

SERVES 4

* 1 large loaf (about 1 lb 12 oz/800 g) soft white sandwich bread, sliced and crusts removed
* 7 oz (200 g) smoked salmon slices (or trimmings)
* 1 cucumber, peeled and thinly sliced
* 4 hard-boiled eggs, shelled and finely chopped
* Handful of chopped chives—with flowers, if possible

For the horseradish mayonnaise

* 4 egg yolks
* 1 teaspoon horseradish sauce
* 1¼ cups (300 ml) cold-pressed rapeseed oil
* 3 teaspoons lemon juice
* Salt and white pepper

PESCATARIAN

For the horseradish mayonnaise, place the egg yolks and horseradish in a large bowl and season generously with salt and pepper (especially salt—I would go with ½ teaspoon). Whisk until completely combined. Now, whisking constantly, add a small drop of oil, then another, and continue, a drop at a time, until the yolks and oil emulsify and start to thicken. At this point, you can slowly start to add more oil, eventually creating a steady, slow stream. Once all the oil has been incorporated, whisk in the lemon juice and adjust the seasoning to taste.

Now assemble layers in an 8-inch (20 cm) square cake pan, ideally a loose-bottom one, being careful to reserve some of the horseradish mayonnaise and cucumber to decorate the sandwich "cake" later. Bread to start, then a thin layer each of horseradish mayonnaise, smoked salmon, cucumber, egg, and chopped chives, followed by more bread with mayonnaise spread thinly on its underside. Repeat until the pan is full, then carefully remove the cake from the pan.

Spread the rest of the horseradish mayonnaise all over the cake, covering it completely. Decorate with cucumber slices and chive flowers, if you managed to procure some. Let your guests admire the beauty of the cake before slicing it into portions to serve.

Parties were thrown here and there,
by the oldster and the black bear,
Bruin, he was always there
and in the feast would gladly share:
He told what he had done and seen,
in the many lands he'd been;
how he'd met a Polish bear
(very respected over there)
who cartwheels, a clever thing,
while carrying a heavy ring,
making it ring merry
all while eating a crimson berry

FROM *BRUIN*,
BY OTTO WILHELM MASING

TARTU:

"CITY OF GOOD THOUGHTS"

Tartu, in Estonia's south, feels like a cozy, creative place built on a human scale. Although it is the country's second-largest city, nothing is too grand here, and even the more majestic buildings feel inviting—some painted in pretty pastel colors, others worn-in and homey.

We were staying among the slightly decrepit, yet utterly charming, wooden houses of Karlova district, which used to be a village outside Tartu but is now a trendy part of town known for its street art. Walking up the staircase to our apartment, it felt as if I had been transported back in time.

At the end of the street was Aparaaditehas ("Widget Factory"), a complex of disused factories with a central courtyard that had been repurposed as artists' studios, vintage shops, boutiques, restaurants, and cafes. Here we soon discovered our favorite breakfast place: at Kolm Tilli, we ate plates of *syrniki* (patties or pancakes made from curd cheese) topped with stewed berries and doused in cream; flatbreads topped with hummus, crispy bacon, avocado, and pumpkin seeds;

and Baltic potato hash alongside perfectly poached eggs draped in hollandaise.

One day, I detected the unmistakable aroma of freshly baked pastries on our street, and it seemed to be coming from somewhere underground. Despite being more than full after eating one of our typically substantial breakfasts, we followed our noses down to a mint-green corridor, with peeling paint, flickering lights, and lots of doors. At the far end were two ladies in hairnets folding what seemed like millions of pastries of assorted shapes and sizes. We mimed our wish to buy some and the women gestured towards a money box by the door. Minutes later, we had four delicious fresh pastries, both sweet and savory, for two euros—surely the best-value lunch in the Baltics!

I had come to Taaralinn—an affectionate name for the city that refers to the pagan god Taara, who was once worshipped in the surrounding oak groves—for a food festival. Among the stalls of braided smoked cheeses and metal barrels of *kvass*, we found the chic women behind Kasekunst birch syrup.

Tartu had the atmosphere of an intellectual monastery—
something hermetic in the best sense of the word.

FROM *THE CAVEMEN CHRONICLE,*
BY MIHKEL MUTT

There's a worn-in feeling to Tartu, like a well-loved
pair of slippers; it feels comfortable and laid back,
never trying too hard to impress.

They patiently and painstakingly explained how the sap was extracted from the birch trees before being transformed into syrup through reverse osmosis. The bread guy sold the most unusual breads (rhubarb rye, anyone?) and at the next stall I met two bright-eyed graduates from culinary school, who, inspired by their travels in Australia, had started a business making salted caramel. A bit further down the street, an Italian cheesemaker married to an Estonian was making Italian-style cheese from local milk, as well as collaborating with his neighbor to produce a cheese marinated in Estonian wine. The stories behind the food were fascinating and uplifting.

The food festival provided a perfect excuse for the inhabitants of Tartu to turn their houses into pop-up cafes—something the Estonians like to do on a regular basis. We stopped at one of these so-called house cafes with masses of balloons outside (there's always some kind of "sign"). On entering the courtyard we were greeted with free homemade cranberry vodka (with seemingly endless refills). At one table there was a man selling fried fish, at another a woman proffered canapes of wild mushrooms and herring on rye bread with lightly brined pickles. When our hosts handed Nusia a whole bunch of balloons, she was overjoyed for about twenty seconds before, perhaps predictably, she lost her grip and the balloons went flying off into the Tartu sky. Equally predictable was the ensuing meltdown.

✳

As we explored the city on foot, drifting between the cobbled streets of its Old Town and the wooden buildings of its outskirts, I immersed myself in its fascinating history. Tartu was born in 600 AD, when settlers built a wooden fortress on a strategically placed hill and called it Tarbatu. In the eleventh century, it was conquered by Yaroslav the Wise, Prince of Kiev, and renamed Yuryev.

Not long after Estonia was declared Christian in 1220—following periods of German and Danish rule—Tartu became the capital of the bishopric of Dorpat, under the control of the Livonian Brothers of the Sword (otherwise known as the Teutonic Knights). By the end of the thirteenth century, Tartu was an important merchant town within the Hanseatic League, a powerful federation of northern German towns and commercial interests with a monopoly on trade in the Baltic Sea. And it was business as usual until the sixteenth century, when the Reformation swept through, Catholic monasteries were closed down, and Tartu was declared Lutheran—some say more on economic grounds than anything else.

Three centuries of relative stability ended categorically when Ivan the Terrible attacked in 1558, his army of Tartars pillaging the countryside and so beginning the Livonian War. But despite Ivan's initial military success, by 1582 Tartu was part of the Polish-Lithuanian Commonwealth, and it was a Polish king, Stefan Batory, who gave Tartu its red and white flag. A turbulent phase followed, with the city repeatedly changing hands between Poland and Sweden, before eventually coming under Russian control early in the eighteenth century. Although there were high points during this time, such as the founding of the prestigious university in 1632, all this conflict took its toll, and Tartu's population fell considerably.

Yet, like a phoenix rising from the ashes, the city rose once more, and by the nineteenth century, it again took its place at the heart of Estonian culture during a time of national awakening, hosting song festivals and the world's first Estonian-language theater. I like to believe that this flourishing sense of identity helped to fortify Tartu—and Estonia—during the trials to come. Two world wars culminated in a regional power struggle between the Nazis and the Bolsheviks, which saw a secret pact promising the Baltics to Soviet Russia (in contravention of an earlier non-aggression pact) and the subsequent mass deportation of Estonians to Siberia.

Despite Estonia's 1918 declaration of independence, it wasn't until the second national awakening, in the late 1980s, that Tartu's flag could be raised again. But somehow, through it all, Tartu has managed to hold on to its soul, thriving as a place of education, creativity, and intellectual freedom—truly a "city of good thoughts."

✳

SOUPS

While in the West we tend to think of soups as something to eat when we feel in need of comfort, warmth, and sustenance, the people of the Baltic region have soups for every occasion.

There are warm soups that nourish and soothe the soul, but equally there are cool soups that will refresh your senses on a swelteringly hot day. There are meaty, umami-rich soups and light, vegetarian ones; there are tangy soups full of fiery ferments and sweet soups packed with seasonal fruit.

My selection on the following pages is just a fraction of what's on offer in the world of Baltic soup. Although these soups are rarely challenging to make, the process can be time-consuming, especially if you make your own stock. Also, many people, myself included, prefer soup after it's spent a day or so in the fridge, when the flavors have had a chance to develop. With this in mind, it makes sense to cook a large pot of soup that you can eat over the next couple of days, and the quantities in the recipes reflect this.

Perhaps the most outstanding feature of the Baltic States is their extensive coastline. As a result, many varieties of fish soup are eaten across the region, but this recipe and the creamy one with dumplings on page 86 are among my favorites—so different from each other that I had to include them both.

I always recommend using sustainable fish from your local area—this will give your soup a distinctive, yet still Baltic, flavor. As a fisherman once explained to me, sustainability depends on where you are, so check with your fishmonger.

BALTIC FISH SOUP

SERVES 8–10

* 1 tablespoon butter
* 1 parsnip, peeled and grated
* 1 carrot, peeled and grated
* ¼ celeriac, peeled and grated, or 2 celery stalks with leaves, finely chopped
* 1 tablespoon tomato paste
* 1 large potato, peeled and diced
* 2 pickles in brine, drained and finely diced
* 1 teaspoon chopped dill, plus extra to serve
* Juice of ½ lemon
* Salt and white pepper
* Sour cream, to serve

For the fish stock

* 1 tablespoon butter
* 1 onion, finely chopped
* 3–6 firm, white-fleshed fish, about 1 lb 5 oz–1 lb 12 oz (600–800 g) in total, gutted but with heads intact
* 1 bay leaf
* 4–5 allspice berries
* ½ teaspoon white peppercorns
* 10½ cups (2.5 liters) water

PESCATARIAN

For the fish stock, melt the butter in a large stockpot over low heat. Add the onion and fry for 2 minutes until soft and translucent, then add the fish, bay leaf, allspice, peppercorns, and about a teaspoon of salt. Pour in the water and bring to a boil. Lower the heat and simmer for 8 minutes, then turn off the heat and remove the fish with a slotted spoon.

Now comes the tricky part: you need to take the fish off the bones, keeping the heads and bones too. Place the fish flesh in a bowl, checking carefully with your fingers for any bones that may have slipped through, and return the heads and bones to the pot. Turn the heat back on and simmer the stock for about 15 minutes. At this point I like to mash the fish heads and bones with a potato masher to get all the flavor out, but if you're feeling squeamish you can skip this part and just cook the stock for an extra 10 minutes.

To make the soup, melt the butter in another, smaller pot over low heat. Add the parsnip, carrot, and celeriac or celery and fry for a couple of minutes until starting to soften, then stir in the tomato paste. Pour in the stock through a fine-meshed sieve (if you didn't go for the mashing option you might want to fish out some of the larger chunks with a slotted spoon first). Add the potato and cook for about 15 minutes, or until cooked but not falling apart.

Now gently stir in the pickles, dill, and lemon juice, along with the reserved fish flesh. Season with salt and pepper to taste, then serve with a spoonful of sour cream and more chopped dill.

My partner is not "a soup person." Whenever I tell him I've made soup for dinner, his face falls as he exclaims sadly, "Ah ... soup." For him, soup is associated with not having enough to eat. Fortunately, this soup is an exception to the rule, and he absolutely loves it—I think it must be all those bite-sized meatballs! Vegetarians can replace them with Green nettle *pelmeni* dumplings (see page 134).

VEGETABLE SOUP
WITH MEATBALLS, FOR NON-SOUP-LOVERS

SERVES 8–10

- 4 large potatoes, peeled and diced
- Squeeze of lemon juice
- 1 tablespoon chopped dill
- Salt and white pepper

For the vegetable stock

- 2 large carrots, peeled
- 1 large parsnip, peeled
- 1 leek
- 2 celery stalks, with leaves
- 1 bay leaf
- 4–5 black peppercorns
- 3–4 allspice berries
- 10½ cups (2.5 liters) water

For the meatballs

- 1 French shallot, very finely chopped
- Rapeseed oil, for frying
- 1 garlic clove, very finely chopped
- 7 oz (200 g) ground beef
- 1 slice of rye bread, soaked in ⅔ cup (150 ml) whole milk
- ½ teaspoon ground cumin
- 1 egg, lightly beaten
- 2 tablespoons all-purpose flour, plus extra for dusting

First, make the vegetable stock. Place the whole carrots, parsnip, leek, and celery in a large saucepan. Add the bay leaf, peppercorns, allspice berries, and about a teaspoon of salt, then pour in the water, bring to a simmer, and cook for 1 hour.

Meanwhile, for the meatballs, fry the shallot in 1 tablespoon of rapeseed oil over medium heat for about 5 minutes or until translucent. Add the garlic and fry for 30 seconds, stirring constantly so it doesn't burn and become bitter. Remove the shallot mixture from the pan and set aside to cool.

Preheat the oven to 200°F (100°C). Dust a large plate with flour.

Place the beef in a large bowl and add the milk-soggy rye bread, cumin, and egg. Combine with one hand, using the other to gradually add the flour. When all the flour is incorporated, add the cooled shallot mixture, season well with salt and pepper, and continue to squish with your hands until everything starts to clump together. With wet hands, form into small walnut-sized meatballs, then roll in the flour on the plate.

Heat a film of rapeseed oil in a large frying pan over medium heat and, working in batches, fry your meatballs for about 10 minutes, turning them regularly, until they are golden all over. Drain on paper towels, then transfer to a heatproof dish and keep warm in the oven while you cook the rest.

When your vegetable stock is done, remove the vegetables with a slotted spoon. Slice the carrot and set aside, discarding (or composting) the others.

Add the potatoes to the pan and cook until they're done—about 15 minutes should suffice—then add the lemon juice and season with salt and pepper to taste. Return the carrots to the pan and stir in the dill.

Place a few meatballs in each bowl and ladle over the soup.

I can't recommend this soup highly enough. An amalgamation of an Estonian fish soup and an old Polish-Lithuanian soup, its dumplings take on the delicate flavor of the stock and practically melt in your mouth.

If you want to make your own fish stock, grab some reasonably priced, locally sourced fish from your fishmonger and follow the instructions on page 84—except there's no need to bother with chopping and frying the onion, you can just add it whole and unpeeled to the pan. Cook the fish in the stock for about 40 minutes before mashing and straining the liquid. You can either discard the strained-out fish or give it to the cat!

CREAMY FISH SOUP
WITH PARSLEY DUMPLINGS

SERVES 8–10

* 1 tablespoon butter
* 2 carrots, peeled and thinly sliced
* 1 leek, thinly sliced
* 1 celery stalk, thinly sliced
* 1 bay leaf
* 4–5 allspice berries
* 10½ cups (2.5 liters) good-quality fish stock
* 1 lb 2 oz (500 g) firm fish fillets, such as salmon or halibut, cut into large chunks
* Generous ¾ cup (200 g) crème fraîche
* Juice of ½ lemon
* Salt and white pepper
* Finely chopped dill, to serve

For the dumplings

* 1 egg, lightly beaten
* 1 tablespoon butter, melted and left to cool slightly
* 3 tablespoons whole milk
* 6 tablespoons all-purpose flour
* 1 teaspoon finely chopped flat-leaf parsley

PESCATARIAN

First make the batter for the dumplings. In a bowl, whisk together the egg, butter, milk, and ¼ teaspoon of salt. Now gradually whisk in the flour to make a smooth batter. Mix in the parsley, then cover and refrigerate while you make the soup.

In a large pot over medium heat, melt the butter and fry the carrot, leek, and celery for 4–5 minutes or until starting to soften. Season with salt and pepper, add the bay leaf and allspice berries, and cover with 8½ cups (2 liters) of fish stock. Bring to a boil, then turn down to a simmer. Add the fish to the soup and cook for about 12 minutes, until the fish is just cooked through.

Meanwhile, cook the dumplings. Pour the remaining 2 cups (500 ml) of fish stock into a small saucepan and bring to a gentle simmer, then drop tablespoonfuls of the chilled batter into the hot stock—the dumplings will float to the surface when they are done. Remove with a slotted spoon and place on a plate.

When the dumplings are ready, put the crème fraîche into a small bowl and stir in a few spoonfuls of the soup (this will help to stop it curdling), then pour into the soup in the pot. Add the lemon juice, season with salt and pepper to taste, and sprinkle with dill.

Place a few dumplings in each bowl and ladle over the soup.

My curiosity was immediately piqued when I came across a recipe for soured wild garlic soup in a local cookbook in Estonia. Hailing from a faraway island off the Estonian coast, this was something I had never tried before. The further I got from my home country of Poland, the less familiar the food seemed to become, although there was always something recognizable about it too—maybe a certain ingredient or flavor—which gave me a strange, dream-like feeling of both knowing and not knowing it at the same time. That was part of the magic of Estonian food for me: familiar, yet different.

This soup is inspired by the one I read about, with fermented wild garlic and buckwheat being the main elements; if you don't want to try your hand at fermenting, you can also buy fermented wild garlic in jars (see page 246).

FERMENTED WILD GARLIC & BUCKWHEAT SOUP

SERVES 8–10

* 5 tablespoons buckwheat (raw or roasted)
* 3 garlic cloves, crushed to a paste with ½ teaspoon salt, using the flat of a knife
* 4 potatoes, peeled and diced
* 5 tablespoons Fermented wild garlic (see page 178)
* Juice of 1 lemon
* Salt and black pepper
* 2 scallions, finely chopped, to serve

For the vegetable stock

* 4 carrots, peeled
* 2 parsnips, peeled
* 1 leek
* ½ celeriac, peeled
* 6 allspice berries
* 10½ cups (2.5 liters) water

VEGAN

In a bowl, cover the buckwheat with water and leave to soak for at least a couple of hours, or overnight.

For the vegetable stock, place the whole carrots, parsnips, leek, celeriac, allspice berries, and about a teaspoon of salt in a large saucepan. Add the water and bring to a boil, then turn down to a simmer and cook for about 40 minutes. Remove the vegetables with a slotted spoon. Slice the carrot and discard (or compost) the rest.

Now add the crushed garlic to the pan, together with the potatoes. Simmer for 10 minutes before adding the fermented wild garlic and cooking for another 5 minutes, or until the potatoes are soft but not falling apart.

Squeeze in the lemon juice, then taste and adjust the seasoning as needed. Finally, add the drained buckwheat, turn off the heat, and let the soup stand for 5 minutes—the buckwheat in the soup is supposed to still be a bit crunchy. Scatter over the scallions and serve.

It seems that every Eastern European country has their own version of sauerkraut soup. Many of them involve pork, which complements sauerkraut beautifully, but I was keen to create a vegan version—partly because I want to tempt everyone to give it a try (I have never met anyone who didn't like sauerkraut soup once they've tasted it), and partly because, given all the other strong flavors here, I don't think meat is necessary. However, if you are an avid meat eater, you could add some pork ribs at the same time as the vegetables.

I like to use my homemade fermented red cabbage for this soup, which I'm convinced is full of the probiotics most beneficial to me (as ferments made in your own environment are thought to be), but of course you could make it with the regular golden sauerkraut available from any Eastern European shop and most supermarkets—just remember to check that it is free of any artificial additives before you buy.

TANGY SAUERKRAUT SOUP

SERVES 8–10

- 1¾ oz (50 g) dried wild mushrooms, such as porcini
- Kettle of boiled water
- 1 tablespoon unsalted butter
- 1 lb 2 oz (500 g) Fermented red cabbage (see page 176) or store-bought sauerkraut
- Salt and white pepper

For the vegetable stock

- 4 tablespoons rapeseed oil
- ½ onion, finely chopped
- 4 medium potatoes, peeled and diced
- 1 carrot, peeled and diced
- 1 parsnip, peeled and diced
- ½ celeriac, peeled and diced
- 1 bay leaf
- 8½ cups (2 liters) water

VEGETARIAN/ VEGAN

Some store-bought dried wild mushrooms are already cleaned, so check the instructions on the package. Otherwise, it's worth giving your dried mushrooms a thorough cleaning to avoid ending up with gritty soup! First, put the mushrooms in a sieve and rinse under cold running water. Pour hot water from the kettle over them to open their cups, and then rinse them under the cold faucet again, rubbing them gently with your fingers. Tip the mushrooms into a heatproof bowl, cover with more hot water from the kettle, and leave to stand for 20 minutes, then drain and return to the rinsed-out bowl. Finally, pour in 2 cups (500 ml) of boiling water from the kettle, cover, and leave to soak for 2 hours or overnight.

For the vegetable stock, heat the rapeseed oil in a large stockpot over medium heat. Add the onion and fry for a minute until just starting to soften, then add the potatoes, carrot, parsnip, and celeriac. Fry the vegetables, stirring constantly, for another minute, then add the bay leaf and pour in the water. Bring to a boil, then turn the heat right down and simmer for 15 minutes.

Meanwhile, melt the butter in a frying pan over a medium-high heat. Drain the mushrooms (reserving the soaking liquid), add to the pan, and fry for 3–4 minutes, stirring constantly.

Tip the mushrooms into the stock, along with their soaking liquid and the sauerkraut, then simmer for another 30 minutes. Season the soup with salt and pepper to taste before serving.

Pork ribs are great for making the sort of hearty soups that are a satisfying meal in themselves, ideally when it's still cold outside. Sorrel comes into season in spring, which is also a good time to forage for young nettle leaves, and you could certainly add some of those to your soup as well. Traditionally, beef stock would be used in a soup like this, but I prefer a lighter chicken stock—I often make it from the carcass of a roast chicken, which I boil with a halved onion and a few bay leaves for a couple of hours, then strain.

This soup is often made with smoked pork ribs. These are not that easy to find outside Eastern Europe, so I like to smoke the ribs myself, using the same method as for smoking fish (see page 56) but with an extra handful of wood chips. Give it a try if you enjoy smoky flavors.

SORREL SOUP
WITH PORK RIBS

SERVES 8–10

* 14 oz (400 g) pork ribs, cut into individual ribs (ask your butcher to do this)—and home-smoked, if you like
* 10½ cups (2.5 liters) good-quality chicken stock
* 2 bay leaves
* 2 garlic cloves, crushed to a paste with ½ teaspoon salt, using the flat of a knife
* 1 cup (200 g) pearl barley, rinsed
* 4 medium potatoes, peeled and diced
* 10½ oz (300 g) sorrel leaves, finely chopped
* Juice of 1 lemon
* Salt and white pepper
* Chopped dill, sliced scallions, and green Tabasco sauce, to serve

Place the ribs in a large saucepan with the chicken stock, bay leaves, and garlic. Bring to a boil, then turn down to a simmer and cook for 1 hour.

Add the barley and cook for 20 minutes before adding the potatoes and sorrel, then keep cooking for a further 15 minutes, until both the barley and potatoes are done.

Squeeze in the lemon juice, then season with salt and pepper to taste.

Serve the soup scattered with dill and scallions—I find that a generous splash of the milder green version of Tabasco sauce makes the perfect finishing touch.

Originating in Russia, *solyanka* gets its name from its saltiness. With the Baltic States having been part of the Soviet Union for so long, there is a clear overlap in terms of cuisine and culture. I like to use oxtail to make this soup, but it does need long, slow cooking, so if you're pushed for time you could choose another cut of beef on the bone, such as short ribs, to reduce the cooking time.

OXTAIL SOLYANKA,
FOR A HANGOVER

SERVES 8–10

* 2½ tablespoons rapeseed oil
* 2 onions, finely chopped
* 2 carrots, peeled and grated
* 4 tablespoons tomato paste
* 3½ oz (100 g) smoked dried sausage, diced
* 10½ oz (300 g) baby potatoes, cut in half
* 2 garlic cloves, crushed to a paste with a pinch of salt, using the flat of a knife
* 2 teaspoons white sugar
* Squeeze of lemon juice
* 6 pickles in brine, drained and finely diced
* 2 tablespoons capers in brine, drained
* Generous 2 tablespoons black olives, pitted and quartered
* Salt and pepper

For the oxtail stock

* 4 slices of oxtail, about 3 lb 5 oz (1.5 kg) in total
* 2 bay leaves
* 15 cups (3.5 liters) water

For the oxtail stock, place all the ingredients in a large saucepan with about a teaspoon of salt. Bring to a boil, then turn down to a simmer and cook for 2½ hours or until the meat is becoming tender. While the stock is cooking, regularly skim off any scum that rises to the surface.

Pour half of the rapeseed oil into a frying pan over medium heat and fry the onions and carrots until soft, then stir in the tomato paste and add to the oxtail stock.

Wipe the frying pan with paper towels and return to medium heat. Pour in the remaining rapeseed oil and fry the smoked sausage until lightly browned on all sides, then add that to the oxtail stock as well.

Now add the potatoes and garlic to the stock, bring it back to a simmer, and cook for 20 minutes or until the potatoes are soft but not falling apart.

Stir in the sugar, lemon juice, pickles, capers, and olives, then season the soup with salt and black and/or white pepper to taste before serving. If you like, you can add a dash of brine from the pickles too (I always do).

If you like the idea of a refreshing chilled soup in the summer months, but you haven't got any fermented beet elixir for the recipe on page 96, then this is another option. If no sorrel leaves are available, you can replace them with spinach and use an extra tablespoon of lemon juice to give your soup that refreshing, sour kick.

REFRESHING GREEN YOGURT SOUP

SERVES 4

* 7 oz (200 g) sorrel leaves, chopped
* 1⅔ cups (400 ml) milk kefir
* 1 tablespoon lemon juice
* 1 cucumber, finely diced (no need to peel)
* 2–3 tablespoons finely chopped dill
* Salt and pepper
* 2 hard-boiled eggs and chopped scallions, to serve
* Ice cubes—optional

VEGETARIAN

Put the sorrel leaves in a large pot and pour in 2 cups (500 ml) of boiling water. Bring back to a boil, then turn down to a simmer and cook for 7–8 minutes until the leaves are tender. Remove from the heat and allow to cool to room temperature.

Add the kefir to the pot, then pulse a few times with a handheld blender—we are not after a completely smooth soup. Add the lemon juice and season to taste with salt and black and/or white pepper (I like to use both).

Place the cucumber and dill in a large serving bowl and pour the soup over the top. Chill in the fridge for at least 30 minutes or up to 24 hours.

To serve, place half a hard-boiled egg in each bowl and ladle over the soup, then scatter with chopped scallions and, if it's a really hot day, ice cubes too.

Cold beet soup is ubiquitous in the Baltics during the summer months, though the details of exactly what goes in and on top of the soup differs from one area to the next. Since I included a recipe for *Chłodnik*, as the soup is known in Polish, in my last book, I had second thoughts when it came to writing about it again—but then I found a new way of making it that I think is worth sharing. Although this version is not necessarily traditional, I love its simplicity and the amazing health benefits it offers. This is cold beet soup on steroids! The only thing here that may seem a bit tricky at first glance is making the fermented beet elixir, but in actual fact it's simplicity itself, so I implore you to give it a shot. The balance between salt and sugar and white pepper is also important: I give my own preferences below but, as always, let taste be your guide.

This soup is a great way of using up leftover cooked potatoes — the contrast between cold soup and warm, slightly crunchy potatoes is close to my heart, as refried potatoes and kefir were a staple snack when I was growing up.

CHILLED KEFIR & FERMENTED BEET SOUP

SERVES 4

- 3½ oz (100 g) radishes, finely diced
- ½ cucumber, peeled and finely diced
- 3 tablespoons chopped dill
- 2 cups (500 ml) milk kefir
- 1⅔ cups (400 ml) Fermented beet elixir (see page 174)
- 1 teaspoon salt
- 1 teaspoon superfine sugar
- ½ teaspoon white pepper
- 2½ tablespoons lemon juice
- Rapeseed oil, for frying
- 2 medium potatoes, peeled, cooked, and diced

VEGETARIAN

Place your radishes, cucumber, and half of the dill in a medium-sized bowl.

Pour the kefir and beet elixir into a jug and mix well. In a small bowl, combine the salt, sugar, pepper, and lemon juice until the salt and sugar have dissolved, then stir into the liquid in the jug. Pour the contents of the jug over the radishes and cucumber and mix everything together very well, then cover and chill in the fridge for at least 30 minutes or up to 24 hours.

Just before serving, heat a little rapeseed oil in a frying pan over medium-high heat. When the oil is hot, add the potatoes and the remaining dill and fry until crisp and golden, stirring regularly.

Taste the soup and adjust the seasoning as needed, then pour into bowls, add the hot dill potatoes, and serve immediately.

The taste of childhood for many who grew up in Eastern Europe, berry soups are always served during the hot summer months. Elsewhere, I'm not sure how this sort of soup might be thought of and eaten—for breakfast, as a snack, or a dessert. To me, it's still undisputedly a soup, so here we are, at the end of the soups chapter: a dessert soup. If you haven't tried this kind of soup before, then you really must, just as soon as the summer berries are ripe and ready. Different berries are used to make soups and there are many variations, but this blueberry version has become a firm favorite of mine.

SUMMER BLUEBERRY SOUP

SERVES 4

* 2⅔ cups (400 g) blueberries
* 1 vanilla bean, split lengthways
* 4 tablespoons sugar
* Generous 1 tablespoon cornstarch
* Whipped cream, torn mint leaves, and edible flowers, such as cornflowers, to serve

VEGETARIAN

Reserve a few of the berries to serve on top of the finished soup, then put the rest into a large pot with the vanilla bean, sugar, and 4¼ cups (1 liter) of water. Bring to a boil, then turn down to a simmer and cook for 15 minutes or until the berries are soft.

In a small bowl, mix the cornstarch with a scant ½ cup (100 ml) of water until smooth. Add this to the pot and stir constantly until the soup thickens. Remove from the heat and allow the soup to cool to room temperature, then chill in the fridge for at least 30 minutes or up to 24 hours.

Ladle the soup into bowls and top with whipped cream, the reserved berries, and a whimsical scattering of mint leaves and edible flowers.

RIGA:

"HOUSE OF HEMP & BUTTER"

Situated close to the mouth of the imposing Daugava River, Riga has long been a bustling trade center (the first record of a harbor here dates back to the second century), and during the early Middle Ages it was a hub of Viking commerce. You could argue that the overall history of the city, a tale of one occupation after another, is encapsulated in its Museum of Occupations.

Officially founded in 1201 by Albert of Buxhoevden as the seat of his bishopric, Riga enjoyed a period of relative stability as a German Hanseatic city until 1581, when it was subsumed into the Polish-Lithuanian Commonwealth. Just forty years afterwards, the Swedes took over, followed by the Russians less than a century later. For years to come, political power in Riga was in Russian hands, while economic might remained largely in the hands of German "Baltic Barons."

In the late nineteenth century, Riga became a focus for the national awakening of Latvian culture, but it would be 1918 before Latvia claimed independence. While the interwar period showed some promise, it was too early to celebrate, and the Soviet annexation of 1940 brought the mass deportations and executions that became known as the "year of terror." Like the unstoppable swing of a metronome, Nazi occupation followed, then the city fell under Soviet control once again, and many Latvians fled to avoid persecution; it would take until 1990 to wrest independence from the occupying forces for good.

✖

With a UNESCO World Heritage-listed historic center and the highest concentration of Art Nouveau buildings in the world, contemporary Riga does not lack gravitas. But another of the city's defining features seems to be that it doesn't take itself too seriously—even its impressive new national library building, known locally as "The Castle of Light," cannot escape the satirist's pen. As Ilza Jansone writes, in her short story "Wonderful New Latvia," "The Castle of Light was built so that it raised itself up over both bridges, every day reminding the people

A city pulsing with energy, Riga kept me constantly entertained with its Art Nouveau architecture, striking contemporary buildings, squares full of summertime flowers, and hip food market.

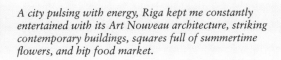

of the meaninglessness and finiteness of their insignificant existence from the past through the present and into the future …" In fact, this imposing building references Latvian legend: a great castle of light is said to have sunk when Latvia was oppressed by other powers, rising again to liberate the nation's people.

Such a metaphor of old wisdom reclaimed is a strong vision for a modern library, and is equally fitting, I feel, when it comes to Latvian cuisine. The recent culinary renaissance has resurrected many old Latvian traditions and given pride of place to local ingredients. In a sixteenth-century Low German song, Riga is described as the "house of hemp and butter"—a description that still feels apt today. Grinding hemp seeds was an ancient way to make a butter that lasted for weeks, if not months, and nowadays it is sold in beautifully designed packaging adorned with golden hemp leaves.

While the iconic Central Market, housed in several hangars, is certainly worth a visit, the young, trendy people congregate at the market in the Kalnciema Quarter. Here, among wooden houses, they eat oysters and drink local beer to a soundtrack of pulsing house music—and it was at this market that I had the best *plov* (pilaf) of my life, made by an elderly Uzbek.

Just like their city, I found Riganites to be open and smart, with a vein of wry wit— qualities shared by two women who cooked me dinner while I was visiting Riga. Linda is a lawyer and food expert, and Madara owns an organic food shop, which means she is familiar with both local trends and wider issues. Faced with so much choice, and the responsibility that comes with that, consumer behavior and attitudes are changing fast in Latvia. She notes: "Five years ago, I had to eat a whole box of artichokes by myself [because no one was buying them] ... now I can sell twenty kilos in a week!"

Together they treated me to a large dose of Latvian hospitality at Madara's airy house on the outskirts of the city. The feast consisted of a flaky-pastry tart of heirloom tomatoes with Latvian green cheese (see page 60 for the recipe), barley porridge with pork lardons and crispy onions, a cucumber and dill salad, roasted buckwheat, and a fish pie made with sprats and fennel. For dessert, my host's

young son served baked apples he had made himself—the image of this serious little boy, dressed in a pale suit, complete with bowtie, squirting whipped cream into the apples, will stay with me for the rest of my days!

✖

Alongside its charming, cobbled Old Town with excellent restaurants, impressive churches, and hidden courtyards, Riga is perhaps most well known for Jugendstil—a dynamic Art Nouveau style that was influential across Eastern Europe in the late nineteenth and early twentieth centuries. As interpreted by local architects, this elaborate style of architecture, inspired by the natural world, says something about the nature of the Latvian people too. Whether living in a busy metropolis, next to a sprawling beach, or in the wild woods, all the Latvians I met on my journey had a deep appreciation of nature in all its facets. Theirs is a spirited energy, one that embraces life with all its complications, darkness and light.

✖

The arches of Riga's railway bridge are echoed in the vast repurposed hangars of its Central Market—Europe's largest—just across the Daugava River.

THE MAIN
EVENT

Bringing ingredients to life is the art of cooking, as described so eloquently by Nora Ikstena in her novel *Soviet Milk*: " ... she was breathing life into it. The pot was simmering away, warmth emanated from the wood stove, the coal and the ribs in the sauerkraut wafted their fragrance."

While chefs in fancy restaurants might pride themselves on composing a work of art on the plate, the less-applauded task of everyday cooking can be just as creative when done with love and care. Although beautifully crafted restaurant meals can be unforgettable, simple home-cooked meals and the feelings they evoke also leave a lasting imprint on our minds and, more importantly, in our hearts.

Rustic, seasonal, and local—whether in restaurants or at home, main meals in the Baltic region tend to be based around simple principles. However this does not mean they are lacking in originality, as ancient ingredients and methods are being used in ever more unique ways, with both a nod to history and a vision for the future.

In this chapter, you will find unique twists on Baltic classics, with plenty of options for meat eaters and avoiders alike! My choice of recipes reflects modern Baltic cooking, rather than the sort of filling meat-heavy cuisine that has tainted the reputation of Eastern European food for far too long.

Smoky roasted buckwheat, or kasha, is a staple across Eastern Europe, and I love to see innovative chefs and cooks giving this traditional ingredient a modern twist, as in this recipe, where it is used as a stuffing for trout or other freshwater fish. Many kinds of freshwater fish are eaten in the Baltic States, and I'm all for widening the range available elsewhere, especially where it could help to take the pressure off our seas.

BAKED TROUT
WITH ROASTED BUCKWHEAT

SERVES 2–4

* ⅔ cup (100 g) roasted buckwheat (kasha)
* 1 carrot, peeled and thinly sliced
* 1 leek, thinly sliced
* Handful of chopped flat-leaf parsley
* 2½ tablespoons cider vinegar
* 5 tablespoons rapeseed oil
* 2 whole rainbow trout, gutted and cleaned
* Juice of ½ lemon
* Salt and black pepper

PESCATARIAN

First, cook the buckwheat: place it in a saucepan with ½ teaspoon of salt and pour in enough cold water to cover by about ½ inch (1 cm). Bring to a boil, then turn the heat right down, cover the pan, and simmer for 20 minutes or until all the water has been absorbed. Remove from the heat and wrap the whole pan, with the lid still on, in a clean tea towel, tying the corners together at the top. Now you want to find somewhere warm: under a blanket and/or cushions—or even in your bed, tucked under the duvet, as my gran used to do! Leave the pan of buckwheat there to rest for at least 30 minutes.

Preheat the oven to 350°F (180°C) and line a baking sheet with parchment paper.

Mix the cooked buckwheat with the carrot, leek, and parsley. Whisk the vinegar with 4 tablespoons of the oil to make a dressing and season with salt and pepper to taste. Pour over the buckwheat and mix well.

Stuff the trout cavities with the buckwheat mixture, then drizzle the remaining tablespoon of oil over the fish and season with salt and pepper. If you have any of the buckwheat mixture left, you can bake it around the trout for a crispy texture, or just eat it as is, alongside the cooked fish.

Bake in the oven for about 20 minutes or until the fish is just cooked—when it's ready, the flesh should be opaque and pull away easily from the bones.

Squeeze over the lemon juice and serve. I like to remove the skin of the trout as I serve it, and save it to make crispy fish skin (see page 142).

The classic Lithuanian *cepelinai* dumplings are usually stuffed with ground meat and served with sour cream and fried bacon bits, so if you're not cooking for vegetarians, feel free to add bacon to the onion topping. Conversely, the dumplings are vegan—it's only the accompanying sour cream that isn't, and you could easily leave it out. Dried lovage (*lubczyk*) is available from all Polish shops, but if you can't get your hands on any, you can replace it with dried oregano.

CEPELINAI POTATO DUMPLINGS
WITH LENTILS & LOVAGE

SERVES 4

* 1 cup (200 g) green or brown lentils, rinsed
* Scant ½ cup (100 ml) rapeseed oil
* 2 onions, thinly sliced
* 1 teaspoon dried lovage (or oregano)
* ½ teaspoon sweet paprika
* 1 x 14 oz (400 g) can of chopped tomatoes
* Salt and white pepper
* Sour cream and sprigs of dill, to serve—optional

For the dumpling dough

* 3 lb 5 oz (1.5 kg) potatoes
* Juice of ½ lemon
* 1 onion
* 2½ tablespoons cornstarch

VEGETARIAN

Cook the lentils in a saucepan of simmering water until tender, about 30 minutes, then drain well.

Pour the rapeseed oil into a frying pan over medium heat, add the onions, and fry for 10 minutes or until golden. Transfer half of the fried onions to a plate and pour most of the oil from the pan over the top.

Add the lentils to the frying pan, along with the lovage and paprika. Stir for a moment, then add the tomatoes. Bring to a simmer and cook uncovered (you want most of the moisture to evaporate) for about 15 minutes, stirring occasionally. Season generously with salt and pepper, then set the filling aside to cool completely.

For the dumpling dough, peel the potatoes, cut into chunks, and place in a bowl of cold water.

Take half of the potatoes and cook them in a large saucepan of boiling salted water until soft but not falling apart. Drain well and mash until smooth.

Take the other half of the potatoes and finely grate them in a powerful food processor or on the smallest holes of a box grater so they turn to mush. Place in a bowl lined with cheesecloth or a clean tea towel and stir in the lemon juice to stop the potatoes from discoloring. Now gather together the corners of the cloth, twist them together, and use your hands to squeeze out the excess water into the bowl. Reserve the soft white starch, which will settle at the bottom of the bowl, just in case you need to use a bit of it to bind the dumplings (usually this isn't necessary, so instead I save the contents of the bowl to pour into my bathwater—it acts as a natural skin softener).

Place both grated raw and mashed potatoes in another bowl. Finely grate in the onion, then season well with salt. Using your hands, mix the potatoes and onion together. Slowly start to add a heaped tablespoon of the cornstarch with one hand while you carry on mixing with the other hand; depending on the potatoes you used, you may not need to use all of it. The aim is to form a ball of soft dough that's neither too wet nor too dry. If the dough feels a bit dry, add a teaspoon or so of the reserved potato starch.

To make the dumplings, take a chunk of the dough—about the size of a tennis ball—and flatten it so that it covers the palm of your hand (as shown in the photograph on pages 116–117). Put a good amount of filling in the middle, a generous 2 tablespoons, then bring up the sides to form a zeppelin shape and pinch together to seal well. Repeat until all the dough and filling is used.

Bring a large pot of salted water to a boil. Mix the remaining heaped tablespoon of cornstarch with about 4 tablespoons of cold water, then add to the pot and return to a simmer.

Working in batches of about four at a time, use a slotted spoon to carefully lower the dumplings into the simmering water and cook for 12–15 minutes. They will float to the top when they are done, but I always give them a few more minutes to make sure they are cooked through.

Meanwhile, put the reserved fried onions and oil into a large frying pan over low heat and fry the onions a little more, until they are crispy.

Remove the cooked dumplings with your slotted spoon, then slip them straight into the frying pan and roll them around in the onions and oil. Serve with sour cream and dill, if desired.

Making Cepelinai potato dumplings with lentils & lovage (page 114)

We were staying in an old wooden townhouse in Liepāja, on the Latvian coast. I had chosen it because of its proximity to a boundless beach with floury dunes, just like those I remember from my childhood holidays on the Polish side of the Baltic Sea. When the owner learned of my food mission, he motioned for me to wait in the courtyard while he ran inside his own house to look for something. Returning with a small, unmarked tin, he explained that his family spent their holidays in the forest, where their neighbor was a hunter. Inside the tin was some recently caught wild boar preserved in oil and spices, which remained in my suitcase for the remainder of the trip. But I had a plan for it ... I knew that when we got home, there'd be no fresh food in the house. However, there's always pasta in the cupboard, tomato paste at the back of the fridge, and thyme in the garden. If you have the time, I implore you to make your own noodles—these ones are based on my grandma's recipe and, uncooked, will keep in the fridge for three days, dusted with flour and stored in a freezer bag or lidded container.

NOODLES
WITH WILD BOAR

Serves 2

- 2 wild boar (or good-quality pork) sausages
- 2½ tablespoons rapeseed oil
- 2 garlic cloves, crushed to a paste with ½ teaspoon salt, using the flat of a knife
- Splash of red wine
- 4 tablespoons tomato paste, mixed with 4 tablespoons warm water
- Handful of thyme leaves
- ¼ teaspoon ground allspice or freshly grated nutmeg
- Salt and black pepper
- Generous 1 tablespoon Latvian green cheese (see page 245) or 2½ tablespoons finely grated hard cheese, such as pecorino or parmesan, to serve

For the noodles

- 1⅔ cups (200 g) all-purpose flour, plus extra for dusting
- 2 eggs

For the noodles, place the flour in a large bowl and add a large pinch of salt. Make a well in the middle and crack the eggs into it, then add about 5 tablespoons of water with one hand while bringing everything together with your other hand. Once you have a rough dough, transfer it to a flour-dusted work surface and knead for 7–8 minutes or until smooth and elastic. Sprinkle your work surface with more flour and use a rolling pin to roll out the dough as thinly as possible. Carefully transfer it to a clean tea towel (if you're finding it tricky to handle the dough, cut it in half before transferring it to the towel) and leave to dry for 2 hours.

Move the dough back onto a flour-dusted surface, sprinkle lightly with more flour, and cut it in half (if you haven't already done so). Taking one half at a time, loosely roll up the sheet of dough, then slice crossways into noodles of the thickness you like. Repeat with the other half of the dough, then shake out the noodles to untangle, spread out, and leave to dry for 30 minutes.

Meanwhile, squeeze the sausage meat out of the casings. Heat the oil in a frying pan over medium heat, add the garlic paste, and fry for 10 seconds. Add the sausage meat and fry, breaking up the meat with a fork, for 3 minutes or until lightly golden. Add the wine to the pan and let it bubble for a moment, then stir in the tomato paste mixture, thyme, and allspice or nutmeg. Season with salt and pepper and let it simmer for 5 minutes or until the meat is cooked through, then adjust the seasoning.

Cook the noodles in a large saucepan of boiling salted water for 5 minutes, until al dente. Using tongs or a slotted spoon transfer them straight into the frying pan. Mix gently with the sauce, then serve immediately, sprinkled with the cheese and more pepper.

While this tart might be inspired by *sklandrausis*—a Latvian sweet carrot tart made with rye pastry, and which is considered almost sacred—I wouldn't dream of calling my recipe that because it is really something quite different. When I was in Estonia, I was served a sort of savory version at a "house cafe" (the Estonians are fond of turning their homes into pop-up cafes), and so my dish is derived from a combination of those two charming carrot tarts, with some coriander thrown in, and a few tweaks to make it vegan.

If you can get hold of rainbow carrots, I suggest you use mostly orange carrots for the tart filling and a mixture of orange, purple, yellow, and white ones on top. You can serve this warm or cold, and it goes very well with the chickpea salad on page 156, which is convenient as the aquafaba used for binding both the pastry and the filling is simply the liquid drained from cooked or canned chickpeas. If you're going to eat the tart as a main meal, some dill-flecked baby potatoes on the side wouldn't go amiss either.

CARROT, CUMIN & CORIANDER TART

SERVES 4

* 13 carrots (ideally rainbow variety), peeled
* 2 medium potatoes, peeled and halved
* 4 tablespoons rapeseed oil
* 1 onion, finely chopped
* 1 garlic clove, crushed
* ½ teaspoon ground cumin
* ¾ teaspoon ground coriander
* 2½ tablespoons aquafaba (see page 245)
* Generous 1 tablespoon orange juice
* Generous 1 tablespoon maple syrup
* Generous 1 tablespoon pumpkin seeds (pepitas)
* Generous 1 tablespoon coarsely chopped cilantro
* Salt and black pepper

For the pastry

* 2 cups (200 g) light rye flour, plus extra for dusting
* 4–5 tablespoons warm water
* 5 tablespoons rapeseed oil
* 1 teaspoon caraway seeds

VEGAN

Cook 9 of the carrots and the potatoes in boiling salted water for 30 minutes or until very soft. Drain thoroughly and mash well.

Heat 2 tablespoons of the rapeseed oil in a small frying pan over medium heat. Add the onion and fry for a few minutes until soft and translucent, then add the garlic, cumin, and ½ teaspoon of the coriander. Fry for another minute, stirring constantly, then stir the contents of the frying pan into the mash. Set aside.

Whisk the aquafaba until it forms soft peaks, like egg whites.

For the pastry, put the flour in a bowl and add ¼ teaspoon of salt. Gradually mix in just enough of the warm water to bring together, then work with your hands until you have a firm dough.

Transfer the dough to a flour-dusted work surface. Add the oil, caraway seeds, and half of the aquafaba and keep kneading for about 5 minutes until you have a smooth ball of dough. Wrap in a clean tea towel and chill in the fridge for 20 minutes.

Preheat the oven to 400°F (200°C) and lightly oil a 10-inch (25 cm) round tart pan, ideally a loose-based one.

Quarter the remaining 4 carrots lengthways and put them in a bowl. Add the remaining 2 tablespoons of rapeseed oil and ¼ teaspoon of coriander, as well as the orange juice and maple syrup. Season well with salt and pepper and toss everything together. Transfer to a baking sheet and roast for 25 minutes, then scatter with the pumpkin seeds and roast for another 15 minutes or until the carrots are tender and the pumpkin seeds are toasted.

Meanwhile, on a flour-dusted surface, roll out the pastry to a ¼ inch (6 mm) thickness, in the rough shape of your pan. Line the pan, easing the pastry into the base and up the sides before trimming off any surplus with a sharp knife. Prick the bottom all over with a fork and bake the tart base for 10 minutes or until lightly golden. Remove and allow to cool slightly, but leave the oven on.

Mix the remaining aquafaba into the mash, then spoon into the tart base and bake for 30 minutes or until golden and set.

Toss the chopped cilantro through the roasted carrots and pumpkin seeds, then arrange in a pile on top of the tart. Serve warm or cold.

Grinding roasted hemp seeds into butter is a traditional Latvian way of creating an oily spread that is both tasty and nutritious. It keeps without refrigeration for a very long time—something I can vouch for, having traveled around the Baltics with some hemp butter (kindly given to me in Riga by my foodie friend Linda) for more than three weeks in the height of summer. Several weeks after my return, we were still eating it at home.

A minute steak needs to be fried very quickly over high heat or it will dry out and become tough, so hemp butter is a great way to inject both moisture and Baltic flavor. Hemp butter is usually made with just hemp seeds, oil, and perhaps a little salt, and so is vegan; however, since the steak means that this meal is definitely not vegan, we can enrich it with a bit of butter—just remember that this will affect its storage qualities and so it probably won't keep as well as the original stuff. If you can't source unhulled hemp seeds, you could use hulled hemp seeds instead and pulse them a couple of times in the food processor, rather than grinding them to a paste.

Roast radishes make a perfect accompaniment, though a green salad or some asparagus always taste great with a steak.

MINUTE STEAK
WITH ROAST RADISHES & HEMP BUTTER

SERVES 4

* 4 x 10½ oz (300 g) minute steaks
* Butter, for frying
* Salt and black pepper

For the roast radishes
* 10½ oz (300 g) radishes
* 2½ tablespoons cold-pressed rapeseed oil

For the hemp butter
* Generous ½ cup (100 g) whole unhulled hemp seeds (see page 245)
* 1½ tablespoons (25 g) butter, at room temperature

Preheat the oven to 350°F (180°C).

Start with the roast radishes. Halve the radishes and place them on a baking sheet, then drizzle with the rapeseed oil and season with salt and pepper. Roast in the oven for 30 minutes, giving them a turn half-way through.

Meanwhile, for the hemp butter, toast the seeds in a dry frying pan over low heat for about 5 minutes, keeping a close eye on them and stirring regularly so they don't burn—they should start releasing a floral fragrance when they're ready. Transfer to a powerful food processor and process until the seeds are ground to a rough paste and have started releasing their oils—you'll know because they'll start to stick to the sides. Add the butter and a large pinch of salt and give everything a final mix, then scrape the hemp butter into a small container and chill in the fridge while you fry the steaks.

Season the steaks with salt and pepper. Melt some butter in a frying pan over medium heat and fry the steaks for about 1 minute on each side for medium, then transfer to a plate, cover with foil, and allow to rest for a couple of minutes.

Serve the steaks with a good dollop of hemp butter on top, the roast radishes, and some blanched or steamed asparagus (or whatever other vegetables you fancy) on the side.

Pork is often associated with Eastern Europe and Germany. In the Baltics, these influences have been strong historically, so pork is commonly eaten at home. It is seen as an everyday meat, whereas game might feature on restaurant menus and is considered to be more for special occasions. Because I don't eat pork very often myself, when I do I like to jazz it up a little, such as with this tangy sea buckthorn sauce; if you can't get hold of sea buckthorn, you could use cranberries instead.

New potatoes with dill make a fresh-tasting accompaniment to these chops, although I have also been known to eat them rustic-style, with buttered crusty sourdough.

CHARRED PORK CHOP
WITH APPLE & SEA BUCKTHORN SAUCE

SERVES 2

* 2 pork chops
* 1 tablespoon butter
* 1 apple, peeled, cored, and diced
* Generous 1 tablespoon honey
* Generous 1 tablespoon cider vinegar
* 1¾ oz (50 g) sea buckthorn berries (see page 246)
* Salt and black pepper

Season the pork chops with salt and pepper. Melt the butter in a frying pan over medium heat and sear the chops for about 4 minutes on each side, until golden brown. Remove from the pan and set aside.

Turn the heat down to low and add the apple, honey, and vinegar to the frying pan, along with 2½ tablespoons of water. Cook for about 5 minutes until the apple is starting to soften, stirring often.

Meanwhile, preheat the broiler to high and line a baking sheet with parchment paper.

Return the chops to the frying pan and cook for 2 minutes on each side, using a spatula to squish them down and move them around the pan. Remove the pan from the heat and stir in the sea buckthorn berries.

Transfer the contents of the pan to the baking sheet and cook the chops under the broiler for a final 2 minutes per side, until they are slightly charred.

They say three's a crowd, yet in the kitchen I find three or four well-matched ingredients are just the right number to make a dish sing. Crispy duck, savory pumpkin, sour redcurrants, and the sweetness of birch (or maple) make up one of my favorite foursomes. Ideally, I would use birch syrup produced in the forests of Estonia (see page 245) for this dish, but if you don't happen to have a bottle of rare birch syrup on hand, then simply use some good-quality maple syrup instead. You can also use fresh cranberries in place of the redcurrants.

CRISPY DUCK BREAST
WITH REDCURRANTS & ROAST PUMPKIN

SERVES 2

- 1 small pumpkin (squash), about 4 lb 8 oz (2 kg), peeled and deseeded
- 1 teaspoon paprika, preferably smoked
- 5 tablespoons rapeseed oil
- 5 tablespoons birch syrup or maple syrup
- 2 duck breasts
- Handful of pumpkin seeds (pepitas)
- Handful of redcurrants
- Salt and black pepper

Preheat the oven to 350°F (180°C).

Thinly slice the pumpkin and place on a baking sheet, spreading out the slices so they will crisp up a little in the oven. Sprinkle over the paprika and season with salt and pepper, then drizzle with the rapeseed oil and birch or maple syrup. Put into the oven to roast.

When the pumpkin has been in the oven for 30 minutes, make a start on the duck. Using a sharp knife, score the skin of the duck breast, being careful not to cut into the flesh. Season the duck with salt and pepper, rubbing it in well.

Place a heavy-based frying pan over medium-high heat and, when it's hot, lay in the duck breasts, skin side down—you won't need any oil. Fry for 3–4 minutes until the skin is crisp and the fat has rendered into the pan, then turn and fry for just 20 seconds on the other side.

Remove the pumpkin from the oven and sit the duck breasts on top, then scatter over the pumpkin seeds and redcurrants. Roast for 10–15 minutes or until the pumpkin is tender and well-browned and the duck is cooked to your liking.

Remove from the oven, cover with foil, and let it rest for about 5 minutes. To serve, transfer the duck breasts to a clean chopping board and slice. Spoon the pumpkin, redcurrants, and pumpkin seeds onto individual plates, then top with the sliced duck breasts.

While beet season may taper off in the depths of winter, this versatile root vegetable stores well and so is generally available year round. Baltic cooking involves a lot of beets, and the bright colors in this "risotto" immediately scream spring to me. At other times of year, however, you could replace the young beet leaves and stalks with about 7 oz (200 g) of spinach leaves—just stir them into the "risotto" near the end of the cooking time. Because I like to use local ingredients, I use crumbly, tangy Lancashire cheese when making this dish at home, but feta or goat cheese work equally well.

SPRINGTIME MILLET "RISOTTO"
WITH YOUNG BEETS

SERVES 4

* 3 young beets, with stalks and leaves
* 4 tablespoons cold-pressed rapeseed oil
* 1 small red onion, finely chopped
* 1¼ cups (250 g) millet grains
* ½ cup (120 ml) white wine
* 4¼ cups (1 liter) hot vegetable stock
* 1 garlic clove, crushed to a paste with a pinch of salt, using the flat of a knife
* 7 oz (200 g) spinach leaves, shredded—optional
* Generous 2 tablespoons chopped dill, plus extra to serve
* Generous 1 tablespoon lemon juice
* 3½ oz (100 g) Lancashire cheese, feta, or goat cheese, crumbled
* 1 tablespoon butter
* 2½ tablespoons Fermented beet elixir (see page 174)—optional
* Scant ½ cup (100 g) sour cream
* Salt and black pepper
* Fermented garlic scapes (see page 179), to serve—optional

VEGETARIAN

Cut the stalks and leaves off the beets, keeping them separate. Roughly chop the stalks and tear any larger leaves into smaller pieces.

Cook the unpeeled beets in a saucepan of boiling salted water for about 30 minutes. Drain and leave until cool enough to handle, then peel and dice the beets. Set aside.

Pour the rapeseed oil into a large frying pan over medium heat. Add the onion and fry for 2–3 minutes until soft and translucent, then add the beet stalks and fry for another minute or so, stirring regularly.

Stir in the millet and immediately pour in the white wine. Let it bubble for a moment to evaporate the alcohol, then add a ladleful of stock and stir until it is absorbed. Keep doing this until you've added about half of the stock, then stir in the garlic. Continue until all the stock has gone—you don't need to stir constantly, just often—and the millet has been cooking for about 15 minutes.

Now add the beet (or spinach) leaves, diced beets, and dill. Keep stirring and cooking until the beets are heated through and the leaves have wilted.

Season with salt, pepper, and lemon juice to taste, then test the millet—if it's not soft enough for you but you've run out of stock, add a little boiling water from the kettle and keep cooking until it is done to your liking.

Finally, stir in the cheese, butter, fermented beet elixir (if using), and most of the sour cream. Sprinkle with the extra dill, scatter with a few fermented garlic scapes (if using), add a final dollop of sour cream, and serve hot.

Tiny Muhu sits huddled next to Saaremaa—Estonia's largest island—and it is often seen as merely a stopover on the way to its bigger, more interesting neighbor. Yet I fell in love with the sparse, minimalistic beauty of this place beyond time, and wished I could have stayed longer. Muhu is known for its orange-and-black ethnic folk art designs and the quality of its lamb. Estonia is generally burger-obsessed, and all the burgers I ate there were excellent; however, it is to Muhu that my mind returns whenever I eat a lamb burger now.

MUHU LAMB BURGERS

MAKES 4

- Rapeseed oil, for frying
- 1 French shallot, very finely diced
- 2½ tablespoons all-purpose flour, for dusting
- 1 lb 2 oz (500 g) ground lamb
- 1 teaspoon smoked paprika
- 4 slices strong cheese, such as Cheddar
- 4 brioche buns
- 2 teaspoons mild mustard, such as Polish *Sarepska* or Dijon
- 4 lettuce leaves
- 1 pickle in brine, drained and sliced
- ½ red onion, thinly sliced and soaked for 20 minutes in lemon juice
- Generous 1 tablespoon diced Fermented celery & carrot (see page 183) or store-bought sauerkraut, well drained
- Salt and white pepper

For the sauce
- 2½ tablespoons sour cream
- 2½ tablespoons mayonnaise
- Handful of finely chopped chives

Heat a little rapeseed oil in a frying pan over medium heat. Add the shallot and fry until golden, then transfer to a large mixing bowl and allow to cool.

For the sauce, combine all the ingredients in a small bowl.

Spread out the flour on a large plate.

Add the ground lamb and paprika to the shallot bowl and season with salt and pepper, then mix with your hands, squishing the meat to bind the mixture together. Shape into four flat patties roughly the same size as your brioche buns, remembering that the burgers will shrink a bit as they cook. Roll the burgers in the flour to coat, shaking off any excess.

Pour a ¼ inch (6 mm) depth of rapeseed oil into a large frying pan over medium heat. Once the oil is hot, add the burgers (depending on the size of your frying pan, you may need to cook the burgers two at a time), and cook for 4 minutes for medium-rare. Turn and cook for 2 minutes on the other side, then top each burger with a cheese slice and cook for another 2 minutes.

Slice the brioche buns in half and spread the bottom half with mustard. Put a burger on each one, then top with a lettuce leaf, pickle slices, soaked red onion, fermented celery and carrot, and some sauce. Cover with the other half of the bun and eat.

Sometimes I enjoy a vegan burger more than a meaty one. Burger joints all over the Baltic States make their vegan burgers using all sorts of meat substitutes, but for me the good old bean burger wins the taste test every time. I find a mixture of beans (dried, not canned) really hits the spot here. I like to use *fasola jaś* white beans, which are available from any Polish shop, though dried lima beans work well too. For me, the ideal topping is some homemade fermented vegetables; however, if you don't have three days to spare to make them, a lovely alternative would be a slice of ripe beef tomato, a few tangy pickle slices, and a few slivers of red onion soaked in lemon juice for about 20 minutes beforehand. And if you are not vegan, you could try a dollop of the pickle sauce on page 136.

BEAN & FLAX BURGERS

MAKES 4

- ½ cup (100 g) dried cannellini beans, soaked overnight
- ½ cup (100 g) dried *fasola jaś* or lima beans, soaked overnight
- 1 large potato, peeled and cut into chunks
- Rapeseed oil, for frying
- 1 onion, finely chopped
- 4 tablespoons ground flaxseed
- 1 teaspoon dried oregano
- 4 slices vegan cheese
- 4 vegan bread buns
- Generous 1 tablespoon mild mustard, such as Polish *Sarepska* or Dijon
- 4 lettuce leaves
- Generous 2 tablespoons diced Fermented celery & carrot (see page 183)
- Salt and white pepper

VEGAN

Drain the soaked beans and cook in a large saucepan of salted boiling water for about 50 minutes, or until soft but still holding their shape. Boil the potato in another pan of salted boiling water until soft but not falling apart.

Meanwhile, heat a little rapeseed oil in a frying pan over medium heat. Add the onion and fry until soft and translucent. Set aside.

Put 1 tablespoon of the ground flaxseed in a small bowl, add 3 tablespoons of water, and allow to stand for 5 minutes—this will be used to bind the burgers. Spread out the rest of the flaxseed on a large plate.

Mash the beans roughly, or pulse them in a food processor, being careful to retain some texture. Mash the potato separately (don't be tempted to use the food processor for this, or the potato will get gluey), then combine with the mashed beans. Add the oregano and fried onion and season to taste with salt and pepper. Finally, add the flaxseed and water mixture and mash everything together again. Shape the bean mixture into four flat patties roughly the same size as your bread buns, then roll the burgers in the flaxseed to coat.

Preheat the broiler to high and line a baking sheet with parchment paper.

Pour a ¼ inch (6 mm) depth of rapeseed oil into a large frying pan over medium heat. Once the oil is hot, add the burgers (depending on the size of your frying pan, you may need to cook the burgers two at a time) and cook for 3 minutes on each side. Transfer the cooked burgers to the baking sheet and top each one with a slice of vegan cheese, then place under the broiler until the cheese melts.

Slice the bread buns in half and spread with mustard. Put a lettuce leaf inside each bun, followed by a burger and some fermented celery and carrot. Cover with the top half of the bun and eat.

This recipe arose from a fish pie made by the lovely Madara, who owns *Unce Eko* organic food shop in Riga, and she in turn was inspired by a traditional fish pie from the Kurzeme region of Latvia, where her mother lives. However, when I tried to recreate it in my kitchen at home, it was impossible: for a start, there were no sprats around at that time of year ... Madara suggested using anchovies instead, so I ran with the idea and transformed the dish into this delicious and fuss-free fish bake.

MADARA'S POTATO, FENNEL & "LITTLE FISH" BAKE

SERVES 4

* 4 large potatoes, peeled
* 2 leeks, thinly sliced
* 1 fennel bulb, thinly sliced
* 2 x 1¾ oz (50 g) cans of anchovies in oil, drained
* Generous 2 tablespoons chopped dill
* Juice of 1 lemon
* Generous ¾ cup (200 ml) heavy cream
* Generous ¾ cup (200 g) crème fraîche
* Coarsely ground black pepper

PESCATARIAN

Preheat the oven to 350°F (180°C) and lightly grease an 8-inch (20 cm) square baking dish.

Cook the potatoes in a saucepan of boiling salted water for 5 minutes, then drain (they won't be fully cooked at this stage, but will finish cooking in the oven). When they are cool enough to handle, cut into thin slices.

Place a layer of leeks and fennel in the base of the baking dish. Scatter with some of the anchovies and dill and season with pepper, then add a layer of potatoes. Keep repeating these layers, squeezing a little lemon juice over each layer, and finish with a layer of potatoes.

Mix together the cream and crème fraîche and season with some more pepper, then pour over everything in the baking dish. Bake for 50 minutes or until golden brown on top and bubbling around the edges.

The dumpling of choice in most of the Baltic States is probably Siberian-style *pelmeni*. Traditionally, these "little ears" are stuffed with meat, but I wanted to update them to reflect the freshness of modern Baltic cuisine. When I made a version with foraged stinging nettles, they were so light and vibrant that each mouthful was like tasting a spring day!

Nettles should be picked in spring, before they flower: you only want the tender tops, usually 5 or 6 leaves per plant, and you will need a big bag of them for the dumpling dough and filling. Make sure you wear sturdy gloves to protect your hands from stings. Outside nettle season, you can use baby spinach leaves instead.

GREEN NETTLE PELMENI DUMPLINGS

SERVES 4

* 2¾–3½ oz (80–100 g) nettle leaves (or baby spinach)
* 5½ oz (150 g) feta or crumbly goat cheese
* Pinch of freshly grated nutmeg
* 1½ tablespoons (25 g) butter
* Salt and white pepper
* Sour cream and finely chopped dill, to serve

For the dumpling dough

* 2½ cups (300 g) all-purpose flour, plus extra for dusting
* 2 egg yolks
* 2½ tablespoons (40 g) unsalted butter, melted

VEGETARIAN

Boil a kettle of water. Wearing rubber gloves (so you don't get stung!), place the nettle leaves in a colander and rinse under cold running water, then pour over boiling water from the kettle to wilt them. Rinse them under cold water again, before gently squeezing out the excess water. Transfer the nettles to a chopping board and chop finely, then set aside.

For the dough, place the flour in a large bowl with a pinch of salt. Make a well in the middle and add the egg yolks, along with 2½ tablespoons of water. Use your hands to start bringing the dough together, gradually adding more water if needed. Finally, work the melted butter and half of the chopped nettles into the dough. Turn out the dough onto a flour-dusted work surface and knead for about 10 minutes until the texture is smooth and supple, like play-dough. Cover with a clean, damp tea towel and allow to rest at room temperature for 20 minutes.

Meanwhile, for the dumpling filling, place the rest of the chopped nettles in a small bowl with the cheese and mash with a fork. Add the nutmeg, season with pepper, and continue to mash until everything is thoroughly combined. Taste to see if it needs any salt.

On a lightly floured work surface, roll out the rested dough very thinly, ideally about 1/16 inch (1.5 mm). Use a round object about 2½–3¼ inches (6–8 cm) in diameter, such as a glass or cup, to cut out circles of dough. Place a teaspoonful of filling in the center of each circle, then fold over to make a half-moon shape and seal by pressing the edges together with your fingers. Now gently wrap the half moon around your finger and press the two outer edges together to seal. Place the finished pelmeni on a flour-dusted surface and cover with a clean, dry tea towel.

When you are ready to cook the dumplings, bring a large saucepan of salted water to a boil and put the butter onto a plate. Working in batches, use a slotted spoon to carefully lower the dumplings into the simmering water. Once they float to the top, give them another minute or two before lifting out onto the plate and coating in the butter. Serve with sour cream and dill.

One of my favorite Estonian supermarket buys was a mixture of "herbs for fish," which inspired this recipe. I suggest you make more of the herb mix than you need here and keep the rest in a jar, ready to use as a dry rub for any fish, especially if it is going to be fried or barbecued.

These herrings go incredibly well with dill-sprinkled potatoes and a slaw (there are four to choose from on pages 148–151).

FRIED HERRINGS
WITH ESTONIAN HERBS, QUICK-PICKLED ONION & PICKLE SAUCE

SERVES 4

- 2½ tablespoons all-purpose flour
- 4 herring fillets
- 2–3 tablespoons rapeseed oil
- Salt and white pepper

For the quick-pickled onion

- 1 red onion, thinly sliced
- Scant ½ cup (100 ml) cider vinegar

For the pickle sauce

- 4 tablespoons sour cream
- Generous 1 tablespoon mayonnaise
- 3 pickles in brine, drained and finely diced

For the "herbs for fish"

- 1 teaspoon dried rosemary
- 1 teaspoon dried parsley
- 1 teaspoon dried basil
- 1 teaspoon dried thyme
- 1 teaspoon dried marjoram
- 1 teaspoon dried oregano
- 1 teaspoon garlic powder
- 1 teaspoon black pepper
- 1 teaspoon salt

PESCATARIAN

For the quick-pickled onion, put the onion in a bowl with a sprinkling of salt. Pour in the vinegar and leave the onion to soak for 20 minutes, then drain.

For the pickle sauce, mix together all the ingredients, seasoning to taste with salt and pepper—just remember to go easy on the salt since the pickles will be salty. Set aside.

To make the "herbs for fish," simply grind all the ingredients to a fine powder using a spice grinder or mortar and pestle.

On a large plate, mix the flour with 1 teaspoon of the "herbs for fish" (the rest will keep for a few months in an airtight container). Dust the herrings in the mixture, coating them on both sides.

Heat the oil in a frying pan over medium heat and fry the herrings for 2–3 minutes each side, or until crisp and golden.

Drain the herrings on paper towels, then serve with the quick-pickled red onion on top and the pickle sauce on the side.

SALADS & SIDES

While Communist-style cooking in the Baltics wasn't exactly known for its salads and vegetable dishes, times have changed. I have a bee in my bonnet about the labeling of Eastern European food as "heavy" and just "meat and potatoes." This is inaccurate, not only in light of all the culinary changes now taking place, but also historically. In the past, fruit and vegetables, both harvested and foraged, were widely appreciated and creatively used in kitchens across the Baltic States, as evidenced by an early-nineteenth-century recipe book published in Lithuania that was one of the first vegetarian cookbooks.

Traditionally, and broadly speaking, in the summer vegetables might be served fresh or simply prepared, while in the winter they would most often be eaten pickled and fermented or used in more hearty dishes, with the addition of meat for extra sustenance. In this chapter, my aim is to inspire you to try Baltic-style salads and side dishes for every season and to suit every palate. Many may indeed be eaten as a light meal in themselves.

The inspiration for this salad comes from a beet and horseradish condiment that is famous throughout Eastern Europe and goes incredibly well with smoked fish. You can hot-smoke your own fish quite easily (see page 56), but store-bought is fine too. And if you're not really a fish person, it's well worth trying the salad, minus the fish, with the chestnut patties on page 57—it makes a brilliant combination. For purely aesthetic reasons, I like to use different-colored beets in this recipe.

They say that food from your immediate environment contains the nutrients your body needs most, so when I have time to forage I like to use wild greens such as dandelion, or nasturtium from the garden, as the base for this salad. Just remember to check that pesticides haven't been used in the area, and make sure you know exactly what you're picking.

SMOKED FISH & BEET SALAD
WITH CRISPY FISH SKIN

SERVES 4

* 4 beets—various colors, if possible
* 2 apples
* Squeeze of lemon juice
* 2 hot-smoked fish fillets, such as salmon or mackerel
* Rapeseed oil, for frying
* Handful of mixed greens
* Handful of Fermented gooseberries or cranberries (see page 182)—optional
* Handful of chopped flat-leaf parsley
* Salt and white pepper

For the marinade

* ⅔ cup (150 ml) cider vinegar
* 1 teaspoon allspice berries
* 1 teaspoon black peppercorns
* 1 bay leaf

For the vinaigrette

* 2½ tablespoons extra-virgin olive oil
* Generous 1 tablespoon lemon juice
* 1 teaspoon horseradish sauce

PESCATARIAN

Combine all the marinade ingredients in a large bowl, then thinly slice 2 of the beets and add to the bowl. Mix well, then leave to marinate for at least 30 minutes or up to 2 hours.

Cook the 2 remaining beets in a saucepan of boiling salted water for about 35 minutes or until soft. When they are cool enough to handle, peel and thinly slice the beets.

Core and thinly slice the apples, then sprinkle with lemon juice so they don't turn brown.

Remove the skin from the fish, then cut it into slivers. Heat a ¼ inch (6 mm) depth of rapeseed oil in a small frying pan over a high heat. When the oil is very hot, add the fish skin and fry for a few minutes until crisp. Drain on paper towels and sprinkle with salt.

Make the vinaigrette by combining all the ingredients in a screw-top jar, along with salt and pepper to taste, and shaking vigorously.

Place a bed of leaves on a serving plate, then arrange the beet and apple slices, and the gooseberries or cranberries (if using), on top. Lay chunks of smoked fish on top of the salad and pour over the vinaigrette, then scatter with the parsley and crispy fish skin.

For many Eastern Europeans, sauerkraut is the taste of home. Luckily, the rest of the world is now starting to recognize the benefits of this magical ingredient, full of probiotics and life! Of course, cabbage fermented at home (see page 176) is best, but you can buy good sauerkraut from any Polish or Eastern European shop—just check the label to make sure it doesn't contain any artificial additives.

Sauerkraut and dill is a quintessential combination, and while it is often paired with meat—usually in the form of crispy pork bits or smoked sausage—I like to make a meat-free version to go with crusty sourdough bread for a light lunch or snack, or with mashed potatoes for dinner.

FRIED SAUERKRAUT WITH DILL

SERVES 4

* 2½ tablespoons cold-pressed rapeseed oil
* 1 onion, finely chopped
* 1 carrot, coarsely grated
* 14 oz (400 g) sauerkraut
* 1 teaspoon runny honey
* White pepper
* Handful of coarsely chopped dill

VEGAN

Heat the rapeseed oil in a frying pan over medium heat. When the oil is hot, add the onion and carrot and fry for a few minutes until the onion is translucent and the carrot is starting to soften.

Stir in the sauerkraut, honey, pepper, and dill and heat just until warmed through. (Unless I'm making a classic Polish *bigos* stew, I never like to cook sauerkraut for too long, so as not to kill the probiotics in it.)

What grows together goes together, as the saying goes ... While chanterelles and blueberries might seem like a cheffy combination—and indeed the first time I tried it was at the elegant Džiaugsmas restaurant in Vilnius—the flavors of the mushrooms and berries felt so natural together that I wondered why I had never eaten the pairing before. A eureka moment!

CHANTERELLES & BLUEBERRIES

SERVES 4

* 1 tablespoon butter
* 10½ oz (300 g) chanterelle mushrooms, cleaned
* 1 large potato, cooked, peeled, and diced
* Scant ½ cup (100 ml) white wine
* Scant ½ cup (100 ml) light cream
* 1 teaspoon mild mustard, such as Polish *Sarepska* or Dijon
* ⅔ cup (100 g) blueberries
* Salt and white pepper

VEGETARIAN

Melt the butter in a large frying pan over medium heat. Add the chanterelles and fry for about 10 minutes, stirring often, until lightly browned. (If your frying pan isn't very big, it's worth doing this in a couple of batches to avoid crowding the pan, or the chanterelles will stew instead of frying.)

Add the potato to the pan of chanterelles and fry for a couple of minutes until golden. Season well with salt and pepper. Stir in the wine, followed by the cream and then the mustard.

Finally, add the blueberries, heat through, and serve. This is divine with nothing more than some fresh bread to dip into the sauce.

I love how the new wave of Baltic restaurants is putting vegetables center-stage. The *White Guide Nordic*, which lists the region's best restaurants, even goes as far as to suggest that spring is the best time to visit northernmost Estonia, because so many restaurants there celebrate the first vegetables of the season.

One prestigious Baltic restaurant is famed for a dish that stuffs a turnip with... more turnip! It's always exciting to see a vegetable as undervalued as the humble turnip get its moment in the limelight. However, stuffing a turnip can be a bit tricky, so I propose something far simpler: a creamy turnip gratin, which is delicious eaten with some slices of Fermented turnip (see page 184) and a green salad.

TURNIP GRATIN
WITH LATVIAN GREEN CHEESE

SERVES 4

* 1 teaspoon butter, softened
* 2½ tablespoons dried breadcrumbs
* Generous ¾ cup (200 ml) heavy cream
* Scant ½ cup (100 g) sour cream
* 1 egg, lightly beaten
* Generous 1 tablespoon mild mustard, such as Polish *Sarepska* or Dijon
* 5–6 medium turnips, about 2 lb 3 oz (1 kg) in total, peeled and thinly sliced
* Generous 1 tablespoon Latvian green cheese (see page 245) or 4 tablespoons finely grated strong cheese, such as pecorino or parmesan
* Salt and white pepper

VEGETARIAN

Preheat the oven to 315°F (160°C). Lightly grease an 8-inch (20 cm) square baking dish with the butter and sprinkle with half of the breadcrumbs.

In a bowl, mix together the cream, sour cream, egg, and mustard. Season with salt and pepper, then beat lightly to combine.

Place a layer of turnips in the bottom of the dish and scatter with some of the cheese. Repeat until all the turnips and cheese are used up.

Pour over the cream mixture, sprinkle with the remaining breadcrumbs, and bake for 40 minutes or until golden brown.

SOME CRUNCHY SLAWS ...

Slaws are as popular in Latvia and Lithuania as they are in neighboring Poland. They should always be left to stand for a while before serving, and because of this they are ideal for a barbecue—you can even prepare them the day before to make life easy for yourself.

What I appreciate most about slaws is their versatility— I generally keep one in the fridge, since I find they go well with almost everything! These slaws are made for sharing, and the recipes on the following pages all make a bowlful for the middle of the table, as part of a spread.

CELERIAC SLAW

MAKES 1 bowlful for sharing

* Handful of walnuts, broken into small pieces
* Handful of pumpkin seeds (pepitas)
* ½ celeriac, peeled and grated
* Handful of raisins
* Handful of finely chopped flat-leaf parsley

For the dressing
* 4 tablespoons sour cream
* 4 tablespoons mayonnaise
* Salt and white pepper

VEGETARIAN

This sweet, earthy slaw is a firm favorite of mine—I often stuff it into warm pita bread for lunch.

Toast the walnuts and pumpkin seeds in a dry frying pan over medium heat for a few minutes, until lightly browned and the pumpkin seeds are starting to pop. Tip into a large bowl and allow to cool, then add the celeriac, raisins, and parsley.

For the dressing, mix the sour cream with the mayonnaise and season very well with salt and pepper.

Pour the dressing into the bowl and mix everything thoroughly, then cover and chill in the fridge for at least 30 minutes (or overnight) before serving.

CARROT & TURNIP SLAW

MAKES 1 bowlful for sharing

* 2 carrots, peeled and cut into thin strips
* 1 medium turnip, peeled and cut into thin strips
* 5 slices Fermented turnip (see page 184), cut into thin strips

For the vinaigrette
* Large pinch of sugar
* 2½ tablespoons cider vinegar
* 5 tablespoons cold-pressed rapeseed oil
* Salt and white pepper

VEGAN

A fresh-tasting slaw (photographed on page 137) that makes an uplifting accompaniment to all kinds of dishes. In Latvia, I ate it with a breaded pork schnitzel and dill-flecked potatoes. The fermented turnip is my own addition—if you don't have any, then just add another small fresh turnip to the mix.

In a screw-top jar, make the vinaigrette by mixing the sugar into the vinegar until it has completely dissolved. Add the oil and shake well to emulsify, then season with salt and pepper to taste.

Place the carrots and turnip in a large bowl and pour over the vinaigrette. Stir to combine, then cover and chill in the fridge for at least 30 minutes (or overnight) before serving.

FIERY RED CABBAGE SLAW

MAKES 1 bowlful for sharing

* 7 oz (200 g) Fermented red cabbage (see page 176)
* 1 red onion, thinly sliced
* 1 apple, peeled, cored and coarsely grated
* 1 red chili pepper, deseeded and finely chopped
* Handful of unhulled hemp seeds (see page 245)
* Finely chopped cilantro, to serve

For the vinaigrette

* 5 tablespoons cold-pressed rapeseed oil
* 2½ tablespoons lime (or lemon) juice
* Salt and white pepper

VEGAN

Photographed on page 137, this red cabbage slaw is the black sheep of the book—my own, rather unconventional take on fermented slaw, it's perfect for when you want a fiery, crunchy addition to your meal. Since I ferment a lot of red cabbage at home, I have had to come up with many ways to use it, and this slaw is perhaps inspired more by my travels in Thailand than in the Baltics. For another Thai element (and as long as you don't need the slaw to be vegan), feel free to add a dash of fish sauce to the vinaigrette.

If you don't have any fermented red cabbage, just use fresh— in which case, you may need a little more vinaigrette. And if you can't get hemp seeds, you can replace them with other toasted seeds, such as pumpkin or sunflower.

In a screw-top jar, make the vinaigrette by combining the rapeseed oil with the lime (or lemon) juice and seasoning well with salt and pepper. Shake well to emulsify.

Place the cabbage, onion, apple, and chili in a large bowl and immediately pour over the vinaigrette. Mix well and chill in the fridge for at least 30 minutes (or overnight).

Just before serving, toast the hemp seeds in a dry frying pan over medium heat for a few moments until they smell toasty. Transfer to a food processor (or mortar and pestle) and grind finely, then scatter over your slaw. Top with cilantro and serve.

FERMENTED BEET SLAW

MAKES 1 bowlful for sharing

* 2 lb 3 oz (1 kg) leftover fermented beets, from Fermented beet elixir (see page 174), grated
* 1 carrot, peeled and grated
* 1 apple, peeled, cored, and grated
* Handful of sunflower seeds

For the vinaigrette

* 4 tablespoons extra-virgin olive oil or cold-pressed rapeseed oil
* Generous 1 tablespoon cider vinegar
* 4 tablespoons sour cream
* Salt and white pepper

VEGETARIAN

Thinking it would be a grave shame to waste the beets left after making fermented beet elixir, I came up with this slaw—it tastes best when left overnight for the flavor to develop.

In a screw-top jar, make the vinaigrette by combining the oil with the vinegar and sour cream. Season well with salt and pepper, then shake well to emulsify.

Place the grated beets, carrot, and apple in a bowl and pour over the vinaigrette. Mix well and chill in the fridge for at least a couple of hours (or overnight).

Just before serving, toast the sunflower seeds in a dry frying pan over medium heat for a few moments until lightly browned, then stir through the slaw.

As I am a great lover of mashed potatoes, I find it hard to resist this Baltic version of British bubble and squeak. I like to eat this with a fried egg on top and something fresh and crunchy on the side. Try my Fiery red cabbage slaw (see page 150) or Beaten-up cucumbers (see page 188) for that palate-cleansing astringent tang, or you could just add a store-bought pickle or two.

BALTIC MASH
WITH BARLEY

SERVES 4

* 1 cup (200 g) barley groats (pot barley; see page 245)
* 2 cups (450 ml) whole milk
* 1 teaspoon dried (or chopped fresh) oregano
* 1 teaspoon dried (or chopped fresh) marjoram
* 2 lb 3 oz (1 kg) potatoes, peeled and cut into chunks
* 1 tablespoon butter
* 3½ oz (100 g) mixed mushrooms, coarsely chopped
* 1 onion, finely chopped
* 6 slices of bacon, cut crossways into strips
* Salt and white pepper

First, wash the barley under cold running water, then place in a bowl, cover in fresh water, and leave to soak for 2 hours.

Drain the barley, then place in a saucepan with the milk and simmer until cooked—this should take about 15 minutes. Stir in the herbs and season well with salt and pepper.

Meanwhile, boil the potatoes in a large pot of boiling salted water until soft, then drain and mash until smooth.

Melt half of the butter in a frying pan over medium heat. Add the mushrooms and fry until browned, then remove from the pan and set aside. Add the remaining butter and fry the onion until golden, then set aside with the mushrooms. Finally, add the bacon to the pan and fry until crisp and golden.

Add the barley to the mashed potatoes, along with the mushrooms, onion, and bacon. Mix well, then gently heat through over low heat before serving.

For many Eastern Europeans, roasted buckwheat is the taste of childhood—and with so many ingredients complemented by its unique smoky flavor, Ottolenghi-style salads using the grain have really taken off in the Baltics in recent years.

The bright orange berries of sea buckthorn are rich in vitamins and have a very particular, sour flavor—if you can't get hold of any, you can replace them in this recipe with the juice of half a lemon. I prefer to use golden and candy-striped beets here, partly for their beautiful array of colors and partly so the whole salad isn't dyed blood-red!

ROASTED BUCKWHEAT SALAD
WITH SEA BUCKTHORN DRESSING

SERVES 4 as a side
or 2 as a main

* 1¼ cups (200 g) roasted buckwheat (kasha)
* 4 medium beets, ideally golden and candy-striped
* ¼ head of red cabbage
* 1 apple, peeled and cored
* Generous 1 tablespoon lemon juice
* 1¾ oz (50 g) pumpkin seeds (pepitas)
* 4 pickles, diced
* Handful of finely chopped dill
* Salt and white pepper

For the dressing

* 1¾ oz (50 g) sea buckthorn berries (see page 246)
* 5 tablespoons cold-pressed rapeseed oil
* Generous 1 tablespoon cider vinegar
* 1 teaspoon mild mustard, such as Polish *Sarepska* or Dijon

VEGAN

Place the buckwheat in a saucepan and pour in enough cold water to cover by about ½ inch (1 cm). Add about ½ teaspoon of salt and bring to a boil, then turn the heat right down, cover the pan, and simmer for 20 minutes or until all the water has been absorbed. Tie a tea towel over the whole pan, lid and all. Now you want to find somewhere warm: under a blanket and/or cushions, or even in your bed, tucked under the duvet, as my grandmother used to do. Leave the pan of buckwheat in this warm place for at least 30 minutes (this will ensure the best texture, which is important in a salad), then allow to cool to room temperature.

Meanwhile, cook the beets in a pot of boiling salted water for about 45 minutes or until tender. Drain and, when cool enough to handle, peel and cut into bite-sized pieces. Place the beets in a large bowl. Finely shred the red cabbage and add to the bowl. Cut your apple into bite-sized chunks, then put it in a small bowl and toss with the lemon juice so it doesn't turn brown.

For the dressing, use a mortar and pestle to crush the sea buckthorn berries. Whisk in the oil, vinegar, and mustard, then season generously with salt and pepper.

Toast the pumpkin seeds in a dry frying pan over medium heat for a few minutes until lightly browned and starting to pop.

Add the cooled buckwheat to the bowl with the beets and cabbage, along with the apple, pickles, and most of the vibrant orange dressing. Gently toss everything together, then sprinkle with the pumpkin seeds and dill and drizzle over the rest of the dressing.

Thanks to the fermented celery and carrot, this colorful, crunchy salad also packs a punch in the flavor department. It's perfect picnic fare—simultaneously filling and fresh. If the mood takes you, feel free to add a handful of cooked beans too; baby broad beans work well, I find.

Remember to save the cooking water from the chickpeas (or the liquid from the tin)—this is aquafaba, and it will keep in the fridge for up to a week. I recommend using it to make Carrot, cumin & coriander tart (see page 120), as it goes so well with this particular salad.

CRUNCHY SALAD OF CHICKPEAS
WITH FERMENTED CELERY & CARROT

SERVES 4

* Generous 1 tablespoon sunflower seeds
* ½ cup (100 g) dried chickpeas, cooked, or 1 x 14 oz (400 g) can of chickpeas
* 5 tablespoons diced Fermented celery & carrot (see page 183), plus 3 tablespoons of the brine
* 1 apple, peeled and finely diced
* 1 orange pepper (capsicum), finely diced
* Handful of salad greens, torn into bite-sized pieces
* Generous 1 tablespoon extra-virgin olive oil
* Salt and white pepper, if needed

VEGAN

Toast the sunflower seeds in a dry frying pan over medium heat for a few minutes until they are lightly browned.

Drain the chickpeas, reserving the liquid (aquafaba) if you want to use it in vegan recipes—it will keep in the fridge for up to a week.

Place the chickpeas in a large bowl and add the fermented celery and carrot, apple, pepper, salad greens, and sunflower seeds. Drizzle over the brine from the fermented vegetables, followed by the olive oil. I find this salad doesn't really need any additional seasoning, but you be the judge.

Often, I am hit with a wave of inspiration when I least expect it. Like when people I've never met come up to me and start telling me their food stories. When I was on TV once, the sound engineer came up to me and began describing a fermented rye and wild mushroom soup his grandma used to make. At a book signing, an elderly lady started reminiscing about a braised nettle salad she used to eat during her childhood in Lithuania. At such times, rather than scrambling for a notepad, I just try to absorb as much as I can in the moment. While the resulting recipes may not be precise, those conversations are engraved in the archive of my mind as "special moments" and I find them a source of endless inspiration.

Nettle leaves should be picked before flowering, making spring the ideal time to make this side dish. If you're not cooking for vegans, it goes well with grilled fish or halloumi cheese.

NETTLE LEAF SALAD

SERVES 4

- 2¾–3½ oz (80–100 g) young nettle leaves (or baby spinach)
- Generous 1 tablespoon sesame or sunflower seeds
- 5 tablespoons cold-pressed rapeseed oil
- 2½ tablespoons lemon juice
- ½ teaspoon mild mustard, such as Polish *Sarepska* or Dijon
- Salt and white pepper

VEGAN

Wearing rubber gloves, pick the nettle leaves from the stems and rinse thoroughly.

Put the nettle leaves in a large saucepan, cover with boiling water, and leave to stand for 2–3 minutes. Rinse under cold water and drain well, using your hands to squeeze out as much water as possible. Shred the nettle leaves and place in a bowl.

Toast the sesame or sunflower seeds in a dry frying pan over medium heat for a few minutes until they are lightly browned.

In a screw-top jar, combine the oil with the lemon juice and mustard, season with salt and pepper, and shake to emulsify. Pour over the nettle leaves and toss gently.

Sprinkle with the sesame or sunflower seeds and serve at room temperature.

I first met Greta in a South London cafe, where we talked about her childhood in Lithuania. She remembers staying at her grandmother's *dacha* (summer cottage), which overlooked the vegetable patch: they used to eat a simple dish of dill potatoes with kefir and fresh vegetables straight from the garden—ripe tomatoes, prickly cucumbers, and scallions. I have also added radishes to the recipe, because I just can't resist tangy kefir with salty radishes.

Sadly, after Greta's grandmother died, the *dacha* was sold, and when Greta and her mother went back to Lithuania to look for it, they couldn't find it anymore.

GRETA'S GRAN'S POTATOES
WITH KEFIR & SUMMER VEGETABLES

SERVES 4

* 1 lb 2 oz (500 g) baby potatoes
* Handful of chopped dill
* 2½ tablespoons cold-pressed rapeseed oil
* 2 ripe tomatoes, coarsely chopped
* 2 scallions, finely chopped
* 2 prickly (pickling) cucumbers or ½ English cucumber, peeled and diced
* 1¾ oz (50 g) radishes, thinly sliced
* ⅔ cup (150 ml) thick milk kefir or kefir yogurt
* Salt

VEGETARIAN

Cook the potatoes in a saucepan of boiling salted water for 15 minutes or until soft but not falling apart. Drain well and leave to cool.

Halve the cooled potatoes, then mix with half of the dill. Pour the rapeseed oil into a frying pan over medium heat and fry the potatoes until lightly browned. Transfer to a serving bowl or platter and set aside while you prepare the vegetables.

In a bowl, combine the tomatoes, scallions, cucumbers, and radishes. Season with plenty of salt, then pour in the kefir and mix gently.

Spoon the vegetables and kefir on top of the potatoes, sprinkle with the remaining dill, and serve.

At the Curonian Spit, a thin strip of land squeezed in between a mirror-still lagoon and a choppy Baltic Sea, we stayed next to the Hill of Witches sculpture park in Juodkrantė. Our surroundings seemed like some kind of exotic layer cake: frothy sea lapped a golden beach flanked by rosehip bushes and fragrant pines, with clusters of pastel-colored houses perched on top like marzipan flowers. In the nineteenth century, the amber-rich lagoon was heavily mined, but these days nearby Amber Bay is populated with ancient symbols instead of excavating machinery, and the Curonian Spit with holiday-makers rather than amber hunters in search of "Baltic gold."

On the banks of the lagoon we ate the most delicious crayfish, simply grilled and served with parsley-butter and lemon. This salad is a homage to that crayfish. If you can't get crayfish tails, the same amount of white crabmeat will work just fine—and canned sweetcorn could be used instead of corn on the cob if you're pressed for time.

CRAYFISH SALAD FROM A LITHUANIAN LAGOON

SERVES 4

* 2 ears of corn,
  or 1¼ cups (200 g) drained canned sweetcorn
* 14 oz (400 g) cooked and peeled crayfish (crawfish) tails
* Olive oil, for drizzling
* Handful of finely chopped flat-leaf parsley
* 2 scallions, finely chopped
* 3½ oz (100 g) mixed salad greens
* Salt and white pepper
* Crusty bread, to serve

For the vinaigrette

* 2½ tablespoons cold-pressed rapeseed oil
* Generous 1 tablespoon lemon juice
* 1 teaspoon mayonnaise

PESCATARIAN

If using corn on the cob, cook in a pot of boiling salted water for 10 minutes or until tender, then drain well. When cool enough to handle, use a sharp knife to carefully slice the corn kernels off the cob.

For the vinaigrette, put the rapeseed oil, lemon juice, and mayo into a screw-top jar. Season with salt and pepper to taste, then shake well to emulsify.

Preheat the broiler to high.

Place the crayfish and corn on a broiler pan or a baking sheet. Drizzle with olive oil and season with salt and pepper, then broil for 2–3 minutes or until they are very slightly charred. Transfer to a bowl and add the parsley, scallions, and most of the vinaigrette. Gently toss everything together.

Arrange some salad greens on each plate and drizzle with the remaining vinaigrette. Place the crayfish mixture on top and serve with crusty bread.

Savory barley porridge is a typical Latvian side dish that is usually combined with bacon, but I prefer to add lots of cheese and serve it with seasonal vegetables on top. In spring, I'd usually go for asparagus, replacing it with purple sprouting or tenderstem broccoli or brussels tops later in the year. You could also use a mixture of greens, of course. If you're a meat eater, feel free to add some crisp bacon bits to your greens too!

What you need for this recipe is barley groats, rather than pearl barley. Its grains are similar in size to couscous, and you should be able to find it in any Eastern European shop (look for *kasza jęczmienna* in Polish shops) and some health food stores.

CREAMY BARLEY GROATS
WITH SEASONAL GREENS

SERVES 4

* 1 cup (200 g) barley groats (pot barley)
* 2½ cups (600 ml) hot vegetable stock
* 1 garlic clove, crushed to a paste with a pinch of salt, using the flat of a knife
* 7 oz (200 g) seasonal greens, such as broccoli or asparagus
* Finely grated zest of ½ lemon
* Handful of hazelnuts, halved
* 1 cup, loosely packed (100 g) grated strong cheese, such as Gruyère or mature Cheddar
* 2½ tablespoons (40 g) butter
* Salt and white pepper

VEGETARIAN

Rinse the barley groats under cold running water, then place in a saucepan with the hot stock. Bring to a simmer and cook for 8 minutes, then add the garlic and keep cooking for another 7 minutes or until the barley is soft.

Meanwhile, place your greens in a frying pan with the lemon zest and a large pinch of salt. Pour in enough boiling water to just cover the greens, then put a lid on the pan and simmer over medium heat for about 5 minutes. Drain in a colander, quickly rinse under cold running water, and drain thoroughly again.

Toast the hazelnuts in a dry frying pan over medium heat for a few minutes until they are lightly browned.

When the barley is cooked, take off the heat. Stir in the cheese and half of the butter, then season with salt and pepper. Cover with a lid and set aside while you gently reheat the greens.

Melt the rest of the butter in a frying pan over medium heat, add the greens and hazelnuts, and fry for a minute or so, just until the greens are warmed through.

Serve the creamy barley groats in bowls, with the greens and hazelnuts on top.

> Laisvės Alėja was being modernized... Asphalt ringed the mature linden tree. The most handsome policemen in the Baltics strode down the boulevard, white-coated hotdog vendors smoked phlegmatically, and famous opera singers paraded by as though in a scene from Othello... And when it got dark, and lanterns lit up the dark halos of the linden trees, groups of streetwalkers poured, like believers on a church feast day, onto the sidewalks...
>
> FROM *WHITE SHROUD*, BY ANTANAS ŠKĖMA

KAUNAS:

BOHEMIAN LIFE & CULTURE

After reading Antanas Škėma's evocative description, I dreamed of visiting Kaunas and promenading along Laisvės Alėja, or Liberty Boulevard, just as the novel's protagonist did in his youth.

Originally constructed by Tsar Nicholas I and named after him, the landmark boulevard was renamed in the interwar period to honor Lithuanian independence (unfortunately this new-found freedom was short-lived, as the onset of World War II saw Lithuania invaded again). During the nineteenth and twentieth centuries, the thoroughfare was a focus of bohemian life in Kaunas: imagine music from gramophones floating through open windows on balmy summer evenings, the sound of lively debate emerging from beautiful little shops and cafes.

But when the magical moment finally arrived, my walk was accompanied by very loud drilling. Fortunately, the boulevard is so long that I still managed to find a quiet spot where I could sit for a few moments in the dappled shade of the linden trees and people-watch—youngsters interacting with their cell phones, older people enjoying a moment of solitude or a rendezvous with friends. There was a sense of anticipation in the air, and I got the distinct feeling that Liberty Boulevard will soon ring with the sound of music once more.

Established in the eleventh century, at the confluence of two rivers, Kaunas became an important trading center in the Middle Ages, but found itself under constant attack by the Teutonic Knights. Even when a castle was built as a deterrent in the fourteenth century, it took until the early fifteenth century to defeat them, after which the town was free to flourish. Having a high proportion of ethnic Lithuanians, Kaunas has long been a focus of nationalist feeling, and the city was the capital of an independent Lithuania from 1920 until Soviet annexation in 1940, growing massively in terms of both population and prestige.

✖

Despite being just an hour's drive apart, Lithuania's two main cities—Kaunas and Vilnius—are quite different in character.

Uncovering the many layers of Kaunas—from the colorful streets of its Old Town to 1930s Modernist architecture and a new wave of street art.

My first impressions of Kaunas were of crumbling churches, a sun-drenched police station with flags fluttering outside, country folk selling jars of wild mushrooms, and youngsters dressed in bold, clashing patterns talking animatedly on street corners. It was also high summer and extremely hot. In short, I felt as if I had arrived in Mexico. Scratch the surface, though, and a new Kaunas emerges: a vibrant city with striking street art, artisan micro-breweries, and small bars branded with hipster-moustache logos; a place with clusters of modern Scandi-style boutiques and vintage shops selling seriously cool clothes from the 1970s and 80s.

An undercurrent of bohemian life still flows through the veins of Kaunas, but it has taken on new forms. Rather than sauntering along Liberty Boulevard, the artists and poets now gather off the beaten track in surrealist cafes, surrounded by street-art murals that are etched like tattoos into the very fabric of the city. Many a nondescript, Communist-style concrete block has been transformed into an imaginative work of art, with the famous pipe-smoking "Wise Old Man" here, and maybe an octopus tentacle or a pink elephant there. Even the old trams are covered in street art.

Contemporary Kaunas is an exciting, constantly evolving city with a rich cultural life. It's also the home of my favorite restaurant anywhere, Uoksas, which I love not only for its brilliant take on modern Lithuanian food, but also for its warm hospitality. Small details stand out, such as offering pre-dinner cocktails that included a non-alcoholic one for three-year-old Nusia. We ate delicate sea bass strips with a cucumber and celeriac sorbet, golf-ball-sized ox-cheek doughnuts with buckwheat, and catfish in a mussel and leek sauce. Nusia wolfed down a massive bowl of crayfish bisque and ate everything on the tasting menu too—definitely a seal of approval! Dessert was "variations on chocolate." Now, I am not usually a great fan of chocolate, but with its melt-in-the-mouth mousse, rich ganache, and crispy cacao nibs, all sharpened by the tartness of summer berries, this luscious dessert won me over completely. While there are many reasons to visit Kaunas, I would deem this restaurant reason enough in itself.

I find it quite extraordinary that there are still places in Europe like Kaunas. It's almost as if they exist in a parallel universe, both remarkably cool and relatively undiscovered. The old-world feel of the city has caught the eye of many directors of period dramas and films over the years, with Pažaislis Monastery being used as a setting for the royal court of St Petersburg, and the ethnographic Open-Air Museum of Lithuania standing in for Belarus in Edward Zwick's 2008 film *Defiance*, and for Tsarist Russia in a television adaptation of *War and Peace*.

With greater exposure coming its way, change is on the horizon for Kaunas, which has been named a European Capital of Culture for 2022. A part of me wants to preserve the faded buildings, garish gangsters, and ancient trams in a time capsule, to lock them away forever and protect them from being blasted by those winds of change. Yet surely Kaunas also deserves its moment in the sun, and to be recognized for the gem that it is.

✖

FERMENTS, PICKLES, PRESERVES

Rarely have I eaten at a Baltic table without there being a little something sour on the side. Pickled and fermented foods are considered a staple—in the past, cold winters could not be survived without them—yet these side dishes and condiments also have the power to transform a lovely meal into a truly memorable one. Fermenting food has become fashionable now that its health benefits have been scientifically proven, but Eastern Europeans have known about these properties for many generations. And anyone who eats fermented foods regularly can attest to their power to make you feel strong and lively!

The process of fermentation is what gives Baltic cooking many of its unique flavors. At Riga's markets you'll find specially prepared bundles of horseradish root, blackcurrant, and wild cherry leaves for fermenting at home. Tannin-rich leaves help to keep fermented and pickled vegetables crisp—in Poland, oak and horseradish leaves are used—but they are by no means essential. However, since the chlorine in tap water can affect the process, it is advisable to use filtered or bottled water, as well as organic vegetables (grown without pesticides or other sprays) and good-quality salt, free of anti-caking agents or other additives. While I've struggled to reproduce some of the more unusual ferments in my faraway kitchen (one day...), simple fermenting really is straightforward. Once you get into it, you will soon be fermenting everything around you, just as Eastern Europeans do.

While you can easily buy ordinary beet juice, this fermented beet juice with garlic is something rather special. It is said that if you drink a shot of this a day, it can help to lower your cholesterol. I like to add a little to beet dishes at the end of cooking, so as not to destroy its health-giving properties—and to make good use of the fermented beets themselves, why not rustle up a bowl of Fermented beet slaw (see page 151).

FERMENTED BEET ELIXIR

MAKES 1 x 1-quart (1-liter) bottle

* 2 lb 3 oz (1 kg) organic beets, peeled and cut into chunks
* 1 head of organic garlic, cloves separated and peeled
* 1 teaspoon good-quality, additive-free salt
* 4¼ cups (1 liter) freshly boiled filtered or bottled water, left to cool a little

VEGAN

First clean your bottle. Either put it through a hot dishwasher cycle or hand-wash in hot, soapy water. Sterilize the clean bottle by submerging it in vigorously boiling water for 10 minutes, then pour out the water and allow to air-dry.

Place the beets and garlic in a ceramic bowl (or a fermenting crock, if you have one), sprinkle with the salt, and pour in the water. Cover the beets with a plate and place something heavy on top, such as a large glass jar, to weigh it down and press out the juice, then leave to ferment at room temperature for 5 days.

Strain the fermented juice through a fine-meshed or cheesecloth-lined sieve into the bottle and seal. It will keep in the fridge for a couple of weeks.

I like to use this red cabbage ferment instead of the more usual, golden-colored store-bought sauerkraut. My young daughter loves it so much she even drinks the brine. Under the illusion that all children must share her tastes, I once gave some to her friend … but that ended in tears!

When the cabbage is young, it releases a lot of liquid by itself as it ferments, but once it's a little older it becomes drier, so you might need to top it up with more brine. Sometimes I add a garlic clove or a slice of apple, but most often I make this, the simplest of recipes. You can, of course, replace the red cabbage with white and still use the resulting ferment in any recipes in this book that call for sauerkraut.

FERMENTED RED CABBAGE

MAKES 1 x 1-quart
(1-liter) jar

* 1 small organic red cabbage, shredded
* About 1½ tablespoons good-quality, additive-free salt
* About 1⅔ cups (400 ml) freshly boiled filtered or bottled water, mixed with 1 teaspoon salt and left to cool until just warm— if needed

VEGAN

First clean your jar. Either put it through a hot dishwasher cycle or hand-wash in hot, soapy water. Sterilize the clean jar by submerging it in vigorously boiling water for 10 minutes, then pour out the water and allow to air-dry.

Weigh the shredded cabbage, then measure out 1½ tablespoons of salt for every 1 lb 3 oz (1 kg) of cabbage. Place the cabbage in a large bowl and add the salt, massaging it in well with your hands. Use a pestle (or a rolling pin) to bash the cabbage for a few minutes until the cabbage softens and releases its liquid. Take a small plate that fits snugly inside the bowl and use it to cover the cabbage, then leave at room temperature for 16–24 hours, pressing down on the plate every time you remember to do so—ideally every hour.

Remove the plate and bash the cabbage with the pestle for about 5 minutes to break down the fibers and release as much liquid as possible. Put the cabbage into the jar, packing it in well, then pour in any liquid left in the bowl and press down firmly again.

If there's enough liquid in the jar to keep the cabbage fully immersed, take a clean weight (I use a scrupulously clean pebble sealed in a small plastic bag) and place it on top. If not, pour in enough of the warm salty water to completely cover the cabbage before adding the weight. Cover the jar loosely with the lid and leave at room temperature for 3 days.

Using a clean fork, scoop out a little of the cabbage and taste to check the level of sourness—if you'd like the flavor to be more intense, you can let it ferment for another day or two.

Once you are happy with your ferment, secure the lid and store in the fridge to use as needed. If you use a clean fork every time and ensure the cabbage remains below the surface of the brine, it should keep well for a couple of months.

Wild garlic (and its North American cousin, ramps) are foraged in spring and I've noticed that they have increased in popularity over the last few years. In the Baltics, I found wild garlic in many dishes. Fermenting means that the use of this delicious green isn't limited to a couple of months of the year, but can be extended into the fall and winter, when a bowl of Fermented wild garlic & buckwheat soup (see page 88) could be just what the doctor ordered.

FERMENTED WILD GARLIC

MAKES 1 x 1-pint (480 ml) jar

* Generous 1 tablespoon good-quality, additive-free salt
* 1⅔ cups (400 ml) freshly boiled filtered or bottled water, left to cool a little
* 3½ oz (100 g) wild garlic leaves (ramsons) or ramp leaves (see page 246)
* 1 organic garlic clove, peeled

VEGAN

First clean your jar. Either put it through a hot dishwasher cycle or hand-wash in hot, soapy water. Sterilize the clean jar by submerging it in vigorously boiling water for 10 minutes, then pour out the water and allow to air-dry.

In a jug, mix the salt into the still-warm water to make a brine, then leave to cool to room temperature, stirring occasionally.

Thoroughly wash the leaves, then pat dry with paper towels. Place the leaves and the garlic clove in the jar, then cover with the brine, making sure they are fully immersed—you may need to weigh them down with a special pickle weight or a scrupulously clean pebble sealed in a small plastic bag.

Cover the jar loosely with the lid and leave it to sit at room temperature for 3–5 days, then secure the lid and store in the fridge to use as needed. If you use a clean fork every time and ensure the wild garlic remains below the surface of the brine, it should keep well for several months.

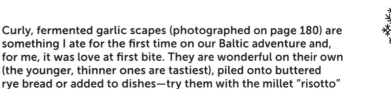

Curly, fermented garlic scapes (photographed on page 180) are something I ate for the first time on our Baltic adventure and, for me, it was love at first bite. They are wonderful on their own (the younger, thinner ones are tastiest), piled onto buttered rye bread or added to dishes—try them with the millet "risotto" on page 128.

Unless you grow your own hardneck garlic, scapes can sometimes be tricky to find: look for them in farmers' markets in their late-spring/early-summer season.

If you live in areas where it grows, you can use foraged three-cornered leek in this recipe, which has a similar garlicky taste when fermented. Do make sure you know exactly what you are picking, though, and triple-check the leaves—they should have three corners, as the name suggests, and will smell of garlic. I like to go foraging for three-cornered leek just before the onset of spring, so the ferment contains flavorsome buds too. I'd recommend letting it ferment for no longer than three days and then keeping it in the fridge for up to a week, whereas garlic scapes can take four or five days of fermenting and will happily sit in the fridge for as long as a month.

FERMENTED GARLIC SCAPES

MAKES 1 x 1-quart
(1-liter) jar

* Generous 1 tablespoon good-quality, additive-free salt
* 2½ cups (625 ml) freshly boiled filtered or bottled water, left to cool a little
* About 9 oz (250 g) organic garlic scapes, trimmed
* 1 organic garlic clove, peeled

VEGAN

First clean your jar. Either put it through a hot dishwasher cycle or hand-wash in hot, soapy water. Sterilize the clean jar by submerging it in vigorously boiling water for 10 minutes, then pour out the water and allow to air-dry.

In a jug, mix the salt into the still-warm water to make a brine, then leave to cool to room temperature, stirring occasionally.

Wash and dry your garlic scapes thoroughly, then lay them horizontally in the jar so that they curl around the sides—this means they should stay in place and you won't need a weight to keep them submerged. Place the garlic clove in the jar, nestling it among the scapes such that they hold it down. Pour in enough brine to fill the jar, cover loosely with the lid, and leave at room temperature for 3 days.

Using clean tongs, take out one of the scapes and taste to check the level of sourness—if you'd like the flavor to be a little more intense, let them ferment for another day or two.

Once you are happy with your ferment, secure the lid and store in the fridge for up to a month, ready to use as needed.

Fermented garlic scapes (page 179)

Fermented red (and white) cabbage (page 176)

Fermented gooseberries
(page 182)

Fermented celery &
carrot (page 183)

181

Picking berries has been part of everyday life in the Baltics for generations, with over twenty types being gathered in Estonia. While this is now mostly a recreational activity and a fun way to connect with nature, historically wild berries were used in folkloric medicine, and during periods of hunger and scarcity they contributed much-needed vitamins to a limited diet. In Communist times, berry picking became an organized group-bonding activity, sometimes at the expense of natural habitats.

Fermented gooseberries (photographed on page 181) are a fantastic way of preserving them for the colder months, but equally they make a welcome addition to meals all year round: try them with cheese on toast or cold cuts, or add them to salads. They do have the potential to become a little mushy as they ferment, so try and get your hands on some tannin-rich leaves, such as oak, horseradish, blackcurrant, wild (sour) cherry, or grapevine; they will help to stop that from happening.

FERMENTED GOOSEBERRIES (OR CRANBERRIES)

MAKES 1 x 1-quart (1-liter) jar

* Generous 1 tablespoon good-quality, additive-free salt
* 4¼ cups (1 liter) freshly boiled filtered or bottled water, left to cool a little
* 1⅓ cups (200 g) organic gooseberries (or cranberries)
* 1 unsprayed tannin-rich leaf, such as oak—optional

VEGAN

First clean your jar. Either put it through a hot dishwasher cycle or hand-wash in hot, soapy water. Sterilize the clean jar by submerging it in vigorously boiling water for 10 minutes, then pour out the water and allow to air-dry.

In a jug, mix the salt into the still-warm water to make a brine, then leave to cool to room temperature, stirring occasionally.

Half-fill your sterilized jar with the gooseberries. Add the leaf, if using, and pour in enough of the cooled brine to cover the gooseberries completely. To keep them submerged, you can either use a special pickle weight or a scrupulously clean pebble sealed in a small plastic bag.

Cover the jar loosely with the lid and leave at room temperature for 3 days. Using a clean spoon, take out one of the berries and taste to check the level of sourness—if you'd like it to be a little more intense, you can let them ferment for another day or two.

Once you are happy with your ferment, secure the lid and store in the fridge to use as needed. If you use a clean spoon every time and ensure the gooseberries remain below the surface of the brine, they should keep well for a couple of months.

Celery isn't a great love of mine, but fermenting transforms what can be a rather bland, watery vegetable into an aromatic wonder! I can't get enough of the fermented stuff, particularly this version with carrot (photographed on page 181), and everyone who tries it has the same reaction—my mama couldn't stop eating this ferment, complete with a look of amazement every time she popped a piece into her mouth.

FERMENTED CELERY & CARROT

MAKES 1 x 1-quart
(1-liter) jar

* Generous 1 tablespoon good-quality, additive-free salt
* 3²/₃ cups (875 ml) freshly boiled filtered or bottled water, left to cool a little
* 6 organic celery stalks, cut into lengths
* 4 medium organic carrots, peeled and cut into chunks
* 2 organic garlic cloves, thinly sliced
* A few organic celery leaves

VEGAN

First clean your jar. Either put it through a hot dishwasher cycle or hand-wash in hot, soapy water. Sterilize the clean jar by submerging it in vigorously boiling water for 10 minutes, then pour out the water and allow to air-dry.

In a jug, mix the salt into the still-warm water to make a brine, then allow to cool to room temperature, stirring occasionally.

Layer the vegetables in the jar, then cover with the brine, making sure they are fully immersed. You may need to weigh them down with a special pickle weight or a scrupulously clean pebble sealed in a small plastic bag, but I find that covering them with celery leaves is usually enough to keep them submerged. Cover the jar loosely with the lid and leave at room temperature for 3 days.

Using a clean spoon, taste to check the level of sourness—if you'd like the flavor to be a little more intense, you can leave the ferment for another day or two.

Once you are happy with your ferment, secure the lid and store in the fridge, ready to use as needed. If you use a clean spoon every time and ensure the vegetables remain below the surface of the brine, they should keep well for about a month.

Ever since I was little, when my mom used to read me the traditional poem about a grandfather whose turnip grew so big that he couldn't pull it up, turnips have been my favorite root vegetable. I love them for both their taste and their association with this story, which takes me back to my childhood.

The turnip is well suited to fermenting. Even without a tannin-rich leaf—oak, horseradish, blackcurrant, wild (sour) cherry, or grapevine—in the jar, it should retain its crunch for at least a couple of weeks. Fermented turnips make an interesting addition to salads and slaws, but it can just as well be served by itself as part of a sharing table.

FERMENTED TURNIP

MAKES 1 x 1-quart
(1-liter) jar

* Generous 1 tablespoon good-quality, additive-free salt
* 3½–3¾ cups (800–900 ml) freshly boiled filtered or bottled water, left to cool a little
* 2 organic garlic cloves, peeled
* 1 unsprayed tannin-rich leaf, such as oak—optional
* 2 organic turnips, peeled and thinly sliced

VEGAN

First clean your jar. Either put it through a hot dishwasher cycle or hand-wash in hot, soapy water. Sterilize the clean jar by submerging it in vigorously boiling water for 10 minutes, then pour out the water and allow to air-dry.

In a jug, mix the salt into the still-warm water to make a brine, then leave to cool to room temperature, stirring occasionally.

Put the garlic cloves in the base of the jar, then drop in the leaf, if using. Layer in the turnip slices and cover with the brine, making sure they are fully immersed—you may need to weigh them down with a special pickle weight or a scrupulously clean pebble sealed in a small plastic bag. Cover the jar loosely with the lid and leave at room temperature for 3 days.

Using a clean fork, taste a slice of turnip to check the level of sourness—if you'd like the flavor to be a little more intense, you can leave the ferment for another day or two.

Once you are happy with your ferment, secure the lid and store in the fridge to use as needed. If you use a clean fork every time and ensure the turnip remains below the surface of the brine, it should keep for at least a month—and if you used a tannin-rich leaf, it will stay pleasingly crunchy.

A popular condiment in both Latvia and Lithuania, as well as parts of Poland, this pickled pumpkin is infused with cloves and allspice for a sweet, aromatic flavor. It makes a distinctive, piquant accompaniment to cheese and cold cuts. This recipe can easily be halved.

PICKLED PUMPKIN

MAKES 2 x 1-quart (1-liter) jars

* 3 lb 5 oz (1.5 kg) pumpkin or winter squash, peeled and cut into chunks
* ½ cup (120 ml) good-quality vinegar, with at least 5% acidity (see note below)
* 5–6 cloves
* 2 allspice berries
* ⅔ cup (120 g) sugar
* 3 cups (700 ml) freshly boiled filtered or bottled water

VEGAN

First clean your jars. Either put them through a hot dishwasher cycle or hand-wash in hot, soapy water. Sterilize the clean jars by submerging them in vigorously boiling water for 10 minutes, then pour out the water and allow to air-dry.

Distribute the pumpkin evenly between the jars, then place all the remaining ingredients in a non-reactive saucepan and bring to a boil. Carefully pour into the jars. Allow to cool fully before covering and storing in the fridge.

Use within 2 weeks.

A NOTE ON VINEGAR

For pickling, I would normally use a vinegar with 10% acidity that I buy from a Polish shop; however, for convenience, you can use any good-quality vinegar with a minimum of 5% acidity, as most white wine and cider vinegars naturally have. The flavor of cider vinegar works particularly well with pumpkin, but may cause the pickled pumpkin to darken slightly—with no ill-effects. If you can source a vinegar with 10% acidity, your pickle should last longer, for up to a month in the fridge.

I use this puree in so many recipes, Baltic and otherwise. As well as adding a bright flavor and plenty of moisture to Pillowy pumpkin buns (see page 28) or Spiced pumpkin cheesecake (see page 196), it also makes a brilliant addition to porridge and dumplings. All in all, it's a great thing to have on hand, and I'm sure you'll soon find your own favorite uses for it.

PUMPKIN PUREE

MAKES 1 x 1-quart (1-liter) jar or container

* 2 lb 3 oz (1 kg) pumpkin or winter squash, peeled and cut into chunks
* ¼ teaspoon salt

VEGAN

Make sure your jar or container is clean and dry.

Place the pumpkin in a pan and pour in just enough water to cover. Add the salt and bring to a boil. Turn the heat right down and simmer for 30 minutes, or until the pumpkin is very soft. Drain well, then transfer to a food processor and process to a puree.

Pour the puree into your container and let cool before covering. Store in the fridge and use within 3 days.

Before fridges and supermarkets made things so much easier, every household had to preserve their own precious meat. As curing fell out of favor in the cosmopolitan cities, it was left to people in the countryside to continue the tradition. Soon the tide turned, however, and now almost every high-end restaurant in the Baltics proudly presents a platter of their own home-cured meat.

This is my uncle's recipe for ham (photographed on page 53), but I use curing salt, which contains antimicrobial sodium nitrite, to be on the safe side—you can get hold of it online. Although the process is a simple one, you'll need to plan ahead as the meat needs 8 days to cure.

EASY HOME-CURED HAM

MAKES about 12 oz (350 g)

* 14 oz (400 g) pork loin
* 2½ tablespoons cider vinegar
* 3½ oz (100 g) sugar
* 3½ oz (100 g) curing salt
* Generous 1 tablespoon dried oregano
* Generous 1 tablespoon dried marjoram

Place the pork loin on a plate, skin side up, and massage the cider vinegar into its skin. Scatter the sugar all over the pork, rubbing it in well. Leave at room temperature, loosely covered with a clean tea towel, for about an hour, rolling it around every now and again to make sure it's completely covered in sugar.

Transfer the pork to a clean tray, cover loosely with the tea towel again, and leave at cool room temperature for 3 days.

Rinse the pork and pat it dry with paper towels, then move the pork onto a clean plate and cover with the curing salt, rubbing it in well. Leave to stand for about an hour, rolling it around in the salt every so often. Transfer to a clean tray, cover loosely with a clean tea towel again, and leave at cool room temperature for a further 3 days.

Rinse and dry the ham, then cover it in the dried herbs. This time, wrap it tightly in a clean tea towel and leave in your kitchen or tie up with string and hang in a cool, dry place for 2 days. The meat will now be a dark pink color.

Store your cured ham in the fridge, where it should keep for about 2 weeks. Serve as part of a cured-meat platter, in sandwiches, or on top of your Baltic wreath (see page 50) if you're after something more fancy.

A NOTE ON MOLD

I have never encountered any mold when curing meat like this, using special curing salt—but if you do, some people swear by wiping the meat with vinegar. I do this anyway, as a precaution, so perhaps this is why I've never had any issues. A light speckling of white mold is usually nothing to worry about, but if you see any green or black mold, I'd advise discarding the meat. And if in doubt, remember it's always best to err on the side of caution. Before you start, it is best to review the National Center for Home Food Preservation website for safe practices.

I was going to call these quick-pickled cucumbers, but they're not actually pickled, just a bit beaten-up!

You will find recipes for pickles in brine in many an Eastern European cookbook (including my own Polish one), so I wanted to provide a quicker, easier option here, especially since I ate cucumbers like this so many times on my travels in Estonia over the summer months, and loved their freshness.

BEATEN-UP CUCUMBERS

SERVES 4

* 1 cucumber or 4–5 prickly cucumbers (these traditional pickling cucumbers are available in most Eastern European shops)
* Generous 1 tablespoon chopped dill
* 1 scallion, finely chopped
* ½ teaspoon caraway seeds— optional
* ½ teaspoon salt

VEGAN

Cut the cucumber into batons, then put into a plastic box with a lid. Add all the other ingredients, close the box and shake vigorously for half a minute or so. Transfer the box to the fridge and chill for about an hour, giving it a shake every now and again.

These pickles should be kept refrigerated, and are best eaten within 24 hours.

This is something my Grandma Halinka, who came from Lithuania, never ran out of. She would have jars and jars of the stuff, carefully stored under a cupboard in her bedroom. When she needed some, she would ask me to fetch a jar for her, a ritual I enjoyed: lying down on the creaky parquet floor and seeing the dark jars lined up against the wall like soldiers, then reaching in and finding one. I'd hand it to her and watch as she opened the jar and dipped in a spoon to check if it was okay (it always was).

My gran ate her plum butter spooned on top of tangy curd cheese, but it's equally delicious as a topping for toast or pancakes and as a filling for all types of cakes and buns. My mama has now taken over the plum butter making tradition, however she likes to put her own spin on it, sometimes adding dark chocolate near the end of the cooking time—delicious!

PLUM BUTTER

MAKES 2 x 1-pint
(480 ml) jars

- ✳ 4 lb 8 oz (2 kg) plums, washed, pits removed
- ✳ 5 tablespoons sugar
- ✳ 2 teaspoons ground cinnamon

VEGAN

Put a tablespoonful of water into a large heavy-based pot, then tip in the plums and sugar. Turn the heat to low and cook, uncovered, for 2 hours, stirring often with a wooden spoon so the plums don't stick to the bottom. Turn off the heat and leave the pot at room temperature, covered, overnight.

The next day, put the pot of plums back over low heat and continue to cook, uncovered, for 1 hour, stirring often. Once again, turn off the heat and leave the pot at room temperature, covered, overnight.

The following day, repeat the plum-cooking process again, this time cooking the plums for 30 minutes. Now add the cinnamon and continue to cook for a final 30 minutes, stirring often. To test if the plum butter is ready, scoop up some of it with your spoon and let it drop back into the pot: if it comes off the spoon in one piece, it's ready; if not, give it another 30 minutes.

Meanwhile, clean your jars. Either put them through a hot dishwasher cycle or hand-wash in hot, soapy water. Sterilize the clean jars by submerging them in vigorously boiling water for 10 minutes, then pour out the water and allow to air-dry.

Transfer the plum butter to the jars while it is still hot. Allow to cool fully before covering. Store in the refrigerator and use within 2 weeks.

If you would like to process this recipe for longer term storage, review the USDA Complete Guide to Home Canning for safe practices.

DESSERTS

Cakes and desserts are much loved by the people of the Baltics—something they share with both their Scandinavian and Polish neighbors. I put it down to climate, with those who live further south in the region less obsessed with sweet treats than their northern counterparts. Somehow, snowy days and cozy dark nights call for hot drinks and comforting cakes. In the balmy days of high summer, on the other hand, desserts tend to contain an abundance of seasonal fruit.

If, like me, you love chocolate mousse but want to try something a bit different, look no further. This mousse is based on a popular dessert called "bread soup"—I found that if you thicken it a little more, it becomes a rich, chocolatey mousse with a hint of rye and caraway. If you're using Eastern European bread, it may well already be flavored with caraway, so you might be able to skip the caraway seeds.

RYE BREAD & CHOCOLATE MOUSSE

SERVES 6

* 10½ oz (300 g) stale dark rye bread, cubed
* ¼ teaspoon caraway seeds, toasted and crushed—optional
* Generous ¾ cup, lightly packed (125 g) soft brown sugar
* Generous 1 tablespoon fine semolina
* 1 cup (250 ml) apple juice
* 3½ oz (100 g) dark chocolate, plus extra to serve
* Generous ¾ cup (200 ml) heavy whipping cream, whipped to stiff peaks

VEGETARIAN

Preheat the oven to 400°F (200°C).

Spread out the bread cubes on a baking sheet and bake for 20 minutes until dried and crisp.

Put the bread and caraway seeds (if using) into a large saucepan, cover with 1 cup (250 ml) of water, and leave to soak for 20 minutes, then add the sugar and bring to a boil, stirring often so it doesn't burn.

Mix the semolina with the apple juice until you have a smooth paste, then add to the pan. Bring to a simmer and stir constantly for about 10 minutes or until it has thickened to the consistency of thick oatmeal.

Break the chocolate into chunks, add to the pan, and stir until melted. Tip the contents of the pan into a food processor and blend until very smooth—this could take up to 10 minutes. Scrape the mixture into a bowl and leave to cool slightly.

Using a large metal spoon, gently fold in most of the whipped cream, saving some for serving, then chill the mousse in the fridge for about half an hour or until set.

Serve with the remaining whipped cream and some shavings of chocolate.

Since cheesecake is said to have originated in Eastern Europe, perhaps it's not surprising that the variety of cheesecakes on offer is astronomical. My current favorite has to be this pumpkin version, with slivers of caramelized pumpkin and melted chocolate sauce to top it off. You can either make your own pumpkin puree or use the store-bought stuff sold in cans for pies—just bear in mind that it will be drier than homemade, so you'll need to use slightly more. And if you don't have any fresh pumpkin to make the topping, you can just scatter some caramelized nuts over the cooked cheesecake.

SPICED PUMPKIN CHEESECAKE

SERVES 10–12

- 3½ oz (100 g) unsalted butter, at room temperature
- 1 cup (200 g) superfine sugar
- 5 eggs, lightly beaten
- 2 cups (500 g) quark (farmer cheese) or cream cheese
- 1⅓ cups (300 g) Pumpkin puree (see page 186) or 1 x 14 oz (400 g) can of pumpkin puree
- Generous 1 tablespoon cornstarch
- 1 teaspoon vanilla extract
- 1 teaspoon ground cinnamon
- Freshly grated nutmeg—optional

For the pumpkin topping

- 1½ tablespoons (25 g) unsalted butter
- 3½ oz (100 g) pumpkin, peeled and thinly sliced
- Pinch of salt
- 5 tablespoons soft brown sugar
- ½ teaspoon ground cinnamon
- ½ teaspoon ground cardamom

For the chocolate sauce

- 3½ oz (100 g) dark chocolate
- 1½ tablespoons (25 g) unsalted butter

VEGETARIAN

Preheat the oven to 350°F (180°C) and lightly grease an 8-inch (20 cm) springform cake pan.

Blend the butter and sugar in a food processor until pale and fluffy then, with the machine running, start alternately adding the eggs and cheese, bit by bit. When all the eggs and cheese are incorporated, add the pumpkin puree, cornstarch, vanilla, and spices and pulse to combine. Scrape the cheesecake mixture into the pan.

Half-fill a heatproof bowl with water and place in the bottom of the oven. Slide the cheesecake onto the middle shelf and cook for 5 minutes, then lower the oven temperature to 315°F (160°C) and cook for 1¼ hours or until barely set. Turn off the oven and leave the cheesecake inside to cool.

Meanwhile, to make the pumpkin topping, melt the butter in a frying pan over medium heat and fry the slivers of pumpkin with the salt, sugar, and spices until caramelized—15 minutes should do it. Set aside to cool.

For the chocolate sauce, melt the chocolate in a heatproof bowl set over a pan of gently simmering water. Stir in the butter to make a smooth, glossy sauce. Allow to cool slightly before using.

When the cheesecake and topping are both completely cool, carefully unmold the cheesecake and transfer to a serving plate, then top with the caramelized pumpkin and drizzle with the chocolate sauce. If you're lucky enough to have any leftover cheesecake, it will keep in the fridge for up to 3 days.

Being a naturally curious person, one of the things I loved most in Estonia were the so-called house cafes: getting the chance to go inside people's homes and eat their favorite dishes was an unexpected highlight of my trip. It was at one such cafe, deep in the countryside, that I ate a cheesecake mixed with an apple tart. I'm not sure if this is a "thing" there, or the host was simply being inventive, but it was so good that as soon as I'd finished, I went back to order another one, in case they ran out …

HALF-&-HALF APPLE CHEESECAKE

SERVES 10–12

- ✳ 1 lb 5 oz (600 g) apples, peeled and diced
- ✳ ½ teaspoon ground cinnamon
- ✳ 2½ tablespoons brown sugar

For the pastry base

- ✳ 2 cups (250 g) all-purpose flour, plus extra for dusting
- ✳ ½ teaspoon baking powder
- ✳ 4½ tablespoons (65 g) cold unsalted butter, cut into cubes
- ✳ ⅓ cup (65 g) superfine sugar
- ✳ 2 egg yolks
- ✳ 2½ tablespoons sour cream

For the crumble topping

- ✳ 5 tablespoons all-purpose flour
- ✳ 2½ tablespoons ground almonds
- ✳ 2½ tablespoons brown sugar
- ✳ ½ tablespoon (10 g) butter

For the cheesecake filling

- ✳ 5½ tablespoons (80 g) unsalted butter
- ✳ ⅓ cup (50 g) soft brown sugar
- ✳ 1¼ cups (300 g) quark (farmer cheese) or cream cheese
- ✳ 2 egg yolks
- ✳ 1 teaspoon vanilla extract
- ✳ 4 egg whites, whisked to stiff peaks

VEGETARIAN

Preheat the oven to 350°F (180°C) and lightly grease an 8-inch (20 cm) springform cake pan.

To make the pastry base, put the flour and baking powder into a large bowl. Use your fingertips to rub in the butter until the mixture resembles breadcrumbs, then add the sugar, egg yolks, and sour cream and bring together into a dough. (Alternatively, just put everything into a food processor and pulse until a ball of dough forms.)

On a flour-dusted surface, roll out the dough to a thickness of about ½ inch (1 cm) and place in the base of the pan, pressing it down gently and evenly. Use a fork to prick the pastry all over, then bake for 15 minutes or until lightly golden.

Put the apples, cinnamon, and sugar into a bowl and toss together. Scatter evenly across the pastry, return to the oven, and bake for 15 minutes or until the pastry is cooked through and the apples are soft. Remove from the oven and allow to cool slightly but leave the oven on, ready to cook the cheesecake filling.

Meanwhile, make the crumble topping by rubbing together all the ingredients with your fingertips until the mixture resembles coarse breadcrumbs. Set aside.

For the cheesecake filling, blend the butter and sugar in a food processor until pale and fluffy. With the machine running, slowly add the cheese, followed by the egg yolks, one at a time. When the cheese and egg yolks are thoroughly incorporated, add the vanilla extract and pulse briefly to combine. Transfer the mixture to a bowl and use a large metal spoon to gently fold in the whisked egg whites.

Spoon the cheesecake mixture into the base, then scatter the crumble topping over the top. Bake for 1 hour or until the filling is just set and the crumble topping is golden brown. Allow to cool in the pan, then carefully unmold and serve.

On our Baltic tour, Riga was by far the most imposing place—everywhere else felt quiet by comparison. And it was here, in the Art Nouveaux district, that my foodie friend Linda took us to a cafe to try the best Latvian rye bread pudding (*rupjmaizes kārtojums*) in the city. It turned out to be like a sophisticated version of trifle, and I ate it with glee, relishing the variety of tastes and textures. This is my interpretation of that dessert, and it's an ingenious way of using up leftover, stale rye bread—just process in a food processor to make breadcrumbs. If the bread you want to use isn't stale, simply dry it out in a 315°F (160°C) oven for 40–50 minutes.

You can serve this as individual trifles in glasses or in one large bowl. For a real centerpiece of a dessert, double the quantities and serve in your best glass dish, as shown here.

LATVIAN RYE BREAD TRIFLE
WITH SUMMER BERRIES

SERVES 4

* 2½ tablespoons unhulled hemp seeds (see page 245)—optional
* 3 cups (400 g) berries, such as strawberries, blackberries, raspberries, and blackcurrants
* Generous 1 tablespoon sugar
* 2 cups (500 ml) heavy whipping cream
* Generous 1 tablespoon confectioners' sugar
* 1 teaspoon vanilla extract
* Edible flowers, such as marigold or apple blossom, to decorate

For the toasted rye breadcrumbs

* 2¾ cups (300 g) rye breadcrumbs
* 2½ tablespoons brown sugar
* 2 teaspoons ground cinnamon

VEGETARIAN

If you are using hemp seeds, toast them in a dry frying pan over medium heat until they smell fragrant, then process in a food processor until finely ground.

Rinse your berries, then drain well, and put into a bowl. Slice any larger berries into halves or quarters. Add the sugar, toss well, and set aside.

For the toasted rye breadcrumbs, mix the breadcrumbs with the brown sugar and cinnamon, then tip into a dry frying pan and toast over low heat, stirring regularly, until crisp—about 15 minutes. Remove from the heat and stir in the hemp seeds, if using.

Whip the cream to soft peaks, then add the confectioners' sugar and vanilla extract and whip to stiff peaks.

Place some of the breadcrumbs in the bottom of each glass, followed by a tablespoon of the sweetened berries, and then half of the cream. (Alternatively, spoon layers of breadcrumbs, berries, and cream into a larger serving dish.) Repeat until everything is used up, finishing with a cream layer, and reserving some breadcrumbs to decorate, then chill the trifle in the fridge for a couple of hours.

Just before serving, add a final scattering of breadcrumbs and decorate with edible flowers.

While this is based on Polish *Pleśniak*, rhubarb and meringue are popular all over the Baltic States, so it feels appropriate to include it here. I originally made the dessert for a supper club and when it quickly became a favorite, I developed this vegan version using aquafaba, or chickpea water.

For the purest flavor, I would recommend making your own aquafaba (see page 245); otherwise, a 14 oz (400 g) can will provide more than enough for this recipe. (The drained chickpeas will keep for a few days in the fridge or several months in the freezer.) If you are not cooking for vegans, you could use three egg whites—one for the pastry and two for the meringue—instead of the aquafaba and replace the coconut oil with the same weight of butter. You can buy rose jam from any Polish shop, or substitute it with any other delicate, fragrant jam such as apricot.

Because it is so moist, this tart (photographed on page 205) keeps well for a couple of days at room temperature.

RHUBARB & ROSE MERINGUE TART

SERVES 10–12

* 1 cup (120 g) walnuts or ¾ cup (120 g) almonds
* Generous 1 tablespoon light brown sugar
* 7 oz (200 g) rose jam
* 14 oz (400 g) rhubarb, rinsed and cut into 1 inch (2.5 cm) lengths
* 1 teaspoon rosewater
* Rose petals, to serve—optional

For the pastry
* 1¼ cups (150 g) all-purpose flour, plus extra for dusting
* ½ teaspoon baking powder
* 1½ cups (150 g) ground almonds
* ⅔ cup (150 g) coconut oil, melted
* 2½ tablespoons sugar
* Pinch of salt
* 4 tablespoons aquafaba, whisked to soft peaks

First make the pastry. Put the flour, baking powder, ground almonds, coconut oil, sugar, and salt into a large bowl. Rub together with your fingertips until the mixture resembles breadcrumbs. Now add the aquafaba and use your hands to bring the dough together. Keep kneading until soft and smooth, then shape the dough into a ball, wrap in plastic wrap (or eco-wrap), and chill in the fridge for 20 minutes.

Preheat the oven to 350°F (180°C) and lightly oil a baking sheet measuring about 12 inches x 8 inches (30 cm x 20 cm).

On a flour-dusted surface, roll out the dough into a rectangle roughly the same size as your baking sheet. Gently lay the pastry in the sheet, pressing it out evenly. Use a fork to prick the pastry all over, then bake for 15 minutes or until lightly golden.

Meanwhile, toast the nuts and brown sugar in a dry frying pan over medium heat, stirring often, until they begin to caramelize. Set aside to cool.

For the crumble topping

* Generous 1 tablespoon all-purpose flour
* Generous 1 tablespoon brown sugar
* Generous 1 tablespoon ground almonds
* Generous 1 tablespoon coconut oil

For the meringue

* 3 tablespoons aquafaba
* 1¼ cups (220 g) superfine sugar

VEGAN

For the crumble topping, put all the ingredients in a bowl and rub together with your fingertips until they resemble coarse breadcrumbs.

Remove the pastry base from the oven and set aside to cool, then turn the oven down to 315°F (160°C).

Next make the meringue by whisking the aquafaba to soft peaks. Slowly add the sugar and keep whisking until you have a smooth and glossy meringue that stands in stiff peaks.

When the pastry base has been cooling for about 15 minutes, spread with the jam. Put the rhubarb in a bowl and toss with the rosewater, then arrange in rows on top of the jam. Place the caramelized nuts in the gaps between the rhubarb. Spoon over the meringue, spreading it out evenly, then sprinkle with the crumble topping.

Bake for 1¼ hours until the meringue is cooked and the rhubarb is tender.

Allow to cool completely in the pan; since this tart is quite wet, you may want to serve it directly from the pan as well. Just before serving, scatter with rose petals, if using.

This malty ice cream is the ultimate fuss-free dessert. Delicious on its own, it's even better with a crunchy topping, like hemp butter or rye breadcrumbs toasted with brown sugar and cinnamon, and it also goes beautifully alongside any warm cake or crumble. Try it with Rhubarb & rose meringue tart (see page 202), as in the photograph here. You don't even need an ice-cream maker or to stir it while it's freezing—the condensed milk takes care of the whole process.

NO-CHURN KAMA ICE CREAM

SERVES 4

* 1 cup (250 ml) heavy cream
* 1 cup (250 ml) condensed milk
* 4 tablespoons *kama* (see page 36)
* Hemp butter (see page 18) or toasted rye breadcrumbs (see page 200), to serve—optional

In a large bowl, whip the cream to stiff peaks. Using a wooden spoon, stir in the condensed milk until well combined.

Stir through the *kama*, then transfer to a lidded plastic container and freeze for at least 3 hours.

Just before serving, crumble over the hemp butter or scatter with the toasted rye breadcrumbs, if using.

Lithuania has a thing about doughnuts. Everywhere I went, there they were—I even ate meat and buckwheat ones! In Kaunas there's a Soviet-style establishment, which serves the best, freshly cooked doughnuts in town for small change. Doughnuts are always best eaten warm—the next day they are nowhere near as good, which I feel is the perfect excuse to have more than one! With these mini ones, you can go wild, but if you do have any left the following day, perk them up by sprinkling them with water and heating in a 315°F (160°C) oven for 10 minutes before serving with some kind of sauce to pour over the top—try using homemade fudge (see page 216) while it's still hot.

ROSE-SCENTED MINI DOUGHNUTS WITH SPICED SUGAR

MAKES 20

- ½ cup (120 ml) whole milk
- ½ oz (15 g) fresh yeast or ¼ oz (7 g) active-dry yeast
- 1¾ cups (220 g) all-purpose flour, plus extra for dusting
- ⅓ cup (60 g) sugar
- ½ teaspoon rosewater
- 4¼ cups (1 liter) rapeseed oil, for deep-frying

For the spiced sugar

- Generous 1 tablespoon confectioners' sugar
- ½ teaspoon ground cinnamon
- ½ teaspoon ground cardamom

VEGETARIAN

Pour the milk into a saucepan and gently heat until it is lukewarm, then remove from the heat and add the yeast, along with a heaped tablespoon each of the flour and sugar. Cover the pan with a clean tea towel and leave in a warm place, such as next to a radiator, for 20 minutes or until frothy.

Meanwhile, sift the rest of the flour into a large bowl and stir in the rest of the sugar. Add the yeast mixture to the bowl, along with the rosewater. Using one hand, work the mixture into dough and bring together into a ball.

Turn out of the bowl onto a flour-dusted surface and knead vigorously for 7–8 minutes, or until smooth and elastic. Return the dough to the bowl, cover with the tea towel, and leave in a warm place for 40–50 minutes or until doubled in size.

Line a baking sheet with parchment paper and dust a small plate with flour. When your dough is ready, take about a teaspoonful and shape it into a walnut-sized ball. Very gently roll it in the flour and place on the baking sheet. Repeat until all the dough is used. Cover the dough balls with the tea towel and leave to rise in a warm place for about 20 minutes or until they have expanded to the size of a golfball.

Pour the deep-frying oil into a high-sided, heavy-based pot and place over a high heat. To test if it's ready, take a scrap of dough and carefully slip it into the oil: if it starts to sizzle immediately and turns golden within 30–40 seconds, your oil is ready.

Working in batches, fry the balls of dough for 3–4 minutes or until puffed up and golden brown, taking care not to overcrowd the pan and turning the doughnuts so they cook evenly. Remove the cooked doughnuts from the oil with a slotted spoon and drain on paper towels while you cook the rest. Keep a close eye on the doughnuts as they cook—remember the oil will get hotter, so later batches may need less time.

In a small bowl, combine the confectioners' sugar with the spices and sift liberally over your doughnuts.

When cooked in the traditional way, on a metal rod over an open fire, this Lithuanian cake looks like a magnificent pine tree: the batter is poured on in layers, with each layer being browned before the next one goes on, to create golden branches. A similar cake is also made in some parts of Poland, where it's known as *Sękacz*, and in many other Eastern European countries. I love this cake so much that I have found a way of making it without all the special equipment, in a bundt pan. It may not be as visually striking as the original, but the taste more than makes up for its looks. And the really brilliant thing about *Šakotis* is that it tastes good even when it has become a little dry, so you can enjoy it with tea or coffee over the course of a few days.

SAKOTIS BUNDT CAKE

SERVES 10–12

* 1 cup (125 g) all-purpose flour
* 1 cup (125 g) cornstarch
* 3 teaspoons baking powder
* 2¼ sticks (250 g) unsalted butter, at room temperature
* 1⅓ cups (250 g) sugar
* 2 teaspoons vanilla extract
* 6 eggs, separated
* Pinch of salt

VEGETARIAN

Butter a 6-cup (1.5-liter) bundt pan and heat the broiler to high.

In a bowl, mix together the two flours and the baking powder. Using a food processor or handheld mixer, beat the butter and sugar until pale and fluffy. Beating constantly, gradually add the vanilla and egg yolks, one at a time, followed by the flour mixture, to make a smooth batter.

In another, clean bowl, whisk the egg whites with a pinch of salt to stiff peaks. Using a large metal spoon, gently fold the egg whites into the batter.

Now put 5 tablespoonfuls of batter into the bundt pan and use a brush to even it out. Place under the broiler and cook until it is a deep golden brown, about 4 minutes. Keep a close eye on it, since it will probably take a little longer at the start, and a little less time as the broiler gets hotter. When the first layer is done, add another layer and cook that too, then keep going until all the batter is used up.

Don't be afraid to properly brown each layer—but if the fierce overhead heat starts to burn the batter without cooking it through (as some broilers can), you might want to switch to using the oven: just preheat it to 425°F (220°C) and continue with the rest of your layers.

After you've cooked the last layer of batter, bake the whole cake in a 315°F (160°C) oven for 20 minutes, then turn off the oven and leave the cake in the cooling oven for a further 20 minutes.

Remove the cake from the oven and let it cool in the pan for 20 minutes, then carefully turn it out while it is still warm and transfer to a cooling rack to cool completely.

In days of old, dried cranberries used to be popular with Baltic sailors, who ate them to prevent scurvy when they were at sea for long periods of time. I could imagine hearty sailors gnawing on salt cod, but cranberries came as a bit of a surprise to me!

In modern-day Latvia I saw ground dried cranberries sprinkled on top of meringues, and so I have used them to create this wintry roulade (photographed on page 211) that's perfect for the Christmas table. Adding some bright red cranberries to the cream gives it a hearty tang and a pretty pink hue.

WINTRY CRANBERRY MERINGUE ROULADE

SERVES 10–12

- 1 cup (175 g) unsweetened dried cranberries (ideally with no added juice or oils)
- Scant ½ cup (100 ml) rum (or cranberry or apple juice)
- 5 egg whites
- 1½ cups (280 g) superfine sugar
- 1 teaspoon vanilla extract
- 1¼ cups (300 ml) heavy whipping cream
- 2½ tablespoons confectioners' sugar
- ⅓ cup (100 g) Greek-style yogurt

VEGETARIAN

Preheat the oven to 375°F (190°C) and line two baking sheets with parchment paper.

Take ¾ cup (125 g) of the cranberries and finely grind in a food processor. Put the remaining (whole) cranberries in a bowl with the rum (or juice) and leave to soak while you make the meringue (no need to soak if your cranberries are soft).

Whisk the egg whites to soft peaks, then slowly whisk in the sugar, adding it tablespoon by tablespoon. Keep whisking until you have a smooth and glossy meringue that stands in stiff peaks. Whisk in the vanilla extract, then spread the meringue onto the baking sheet to a thickness of about ½ inch (1 cm).

Bake for 8 minutes, then turn the oven down to 300°F (150°C) and bake for a further 15 minutes until crisp. Remove from the oven and allow to cool for 5 minutes, then carefully turn the meringue upside down onto the other lined baking sheet and leave to cool for 15 minutes.

Meanwhile, whip the cream to soft peaks, then add 1 heaped tablespoon of the confectioners' sugar and whip to incorporate. Using a large metal spoon, gently fold in the yogurt, followed by a tablespoon of the ground cranberries and all of the drained soaked cranberries.

Spread the cranberry cream onto the meringue, leaving a ¾-inch (2 cm) border all around the edges. Starting at one of the shorter sides, carefully roll up the meringue, using the parchment paper to help you.

Chill the roulade for at least an hour, then sift the remaining confectioners' sugar over the top and sprinkle with the remaininig ground cranberry powder.

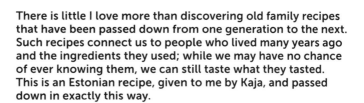

There is little I love more than discovering old family recipes that have been passed down from one generation to the next. Such recipes connect us to people who lived many years ago and the ingredients they used; while we may have no chance of ever knowing them, we can still taste what they tasted. This is an Estonian recipe, given to me by Kaja, and passed down in exactly this way.

I met Kaja on my travels through the country and she kindly welcomed me into her home, where she plied me with poppyseed pastries, berries, this sour milk dessert, and food stories. The story surrounding this particular dish (photographed on pages 210–211) goes that whenever a son in the family brought home a girl he was planning to marry, she would be "tested" with this dessert. If she liked the "sour milk lady," then she passed. Well, I would have won this test hands down, because I ended up eating two at Kaja's house! As the name suggests, originally this dessert was made with sour milk, however Kaja sometimes uses kefir now; the vanilla is my addition.

KAJA'S "SOUR MILK LADY"
WITH BERRIES

SERVES 6

* 4¼ cups (1 liter) milk kefir
* ¾ cup (100 g) all-purpose flour
* ¾ cup (150 g) sugar
* 1 vanilla bean—optional
* 2¼ cups (300 g) mixed berries, such as strawberries, raspberries, blackberries, and blueberries
* Handful of mint leaves, torn

VEGETARIAN

Put ¼ cup (60 ml) of the kefir into a large saucepan, add 2 tablespoons of the flour, and stir until smooth. Add the rest of the kefir and flour, along with the sugar, and stir until there are no lumps. If using the vanilla bean, split it lengthways, then scrape the seeds out of the pod with the tip of a knife and add to the pan. Bring to a boil over medium heat, stirring every minute or so. When bubbles start to appear, turn the heat right down and stir constantly as it thickens and becomes creamy.

Once the mixture has the consistency of thick custard, pour into six glass dishes, leaving enough room at the top for the berries. Allow to cool at room temperature, then chill in the fridge until ready to serve.

Just before serving, quarter the strawberries, then combine with the other berries. Top your "sour milk lady" with the berries and some torn mint leaves.

Greta's medutis
honey layer cake
(page 212)

Kaja's "sour milk
lady" with berries
(page 209)

Wintry cranberry meringue roulade (page 208)

211

Lithuanian is an ancient language that has been preserved through a rich oral tradition. It sounds beautiful to my ears, therefore I have gone with the Lithuanian name for this cake, *Medutis*, rather than the more common, Russian *Medovik* or Polish *Miodownik*. Known all over Eastern Europe in various guises, some say it was invented in the early nineteenth century in the court of Tsar Alexander the Great, while others claim its roots to be Ashkenazi Jewish.

Greta grew up in a fairly traditional Lithuanian family. She remembers going to church on Sundays with her mom, and afterwards they would go to a cafe for a slice of her favorite *Medutis* honey layer cake. This is Greta's take on that cake (photographed on page 210), which I happen to love. You'll need to start this recipe the day before, since the finished cake requires overnight chilling.

GRETA'S MEDUTIS HONEY LAYER CAKE

SERVES 8–10

* ½ cup (150 g) blossom honey
* 1 stick (115 g) unsalted butter
* 1 cup, lightly packed (150 g) light brown sugar
* 1 teaspoon ground cinnamon
* ½ teaspoon freshly grated nutmeg
* ½ teaspoon finely ground black pepper
* ¼ teaspoon ground cloves
* 4 cups (500 g) all-purpose flour, plus extra for dusting
* 1 teaspoon baking powder
* 3 large eggs, lightly beaten
* Pinch of salt
* Handful of toasted almonds
* Finely grated lemon zest, to serve

For the filling

* 3¾ cups (900 g) crème fraîche
* ⅔ cup (120 g) superfine sugar
* 1 teaspoon vanilla extract
* Finely grated zest of 1 lemon
* 2½ tablespoons lemon juice
* Generous ¾ cup (200 ml) heavy cream

Put the honey into a small, heavy-based saucepan and cook over medium heat for 5–10 minutes or until it turns a couple of shades darker. Watch it carefully—there should be lots of bubbles but no smoke! Set aside to cool.

Add the butter and sugar to the cooled honey and return the pan to medium heat. Cook for 3 minutes, then stir in the spices and cook for another 2 minutes, or until the butter has melted and the sugar has dissolved. Pour into a large heatproof bowl and leave to cool for about 15 minutes.

Meanwhile, sift 3¾ cups (470 g) of the flour and the baking powder into another bowl.

Slowly add the beaten egg to the honey mixture, while whisking continuously. When it has all been incorporated, start adding the flour mixture and salt, mixing well as you go, until you have something like a sticky cookie dough.

Preheat the oven to 400°F (200°C). Take as many baking sheets as you can fit into the oven at once and line each one with a sheet of parchment paper.

Dust your work surface heavily with flour and knead the dough until it becomes soft and pillowy, adding flour as needed to make it more manageable—just keep in mind that using the least amount of flour possible will result in lighter, fluffier layers of cake.

While the dough is still a little warm, divide it into 8 equal portions. Work with one portion of dough at a time, keeping the rest covered with damp paper towel. Place it on one of the sheets of parchment paper, dust lightly with flour, and roll out into a very thin rectangle slightly bigger than the base of a 1 lb (450 g) loaf pan.

For the mascarpone cream

* 2½ tablespoons confectioners' sugar
* 1 cup (250 g) mascarpone
* Scant ½ cup (100 ml) heavy whipping cream, chilled
* Squeeze of lemon juice

VEGETARIAN

Carefully transfer to one of the baking sheets and trim to the correct size for your loaf pan, saving all the trimmings. Don't worry if you get any holes—just patch up with some of the trimmings once it is safely on the baking sheet.

When you have rolled out as many rectangles of dough as you can fit in the oven at once, bake for 8–9 minutes or until starting to brown slightly around the edges—when they are done, they should be like gingerbread cookies. Transfer to wire racks and leave to cool while you roll out and bake the rest.

Gather all the remaining trimmings of dough, place on a paper-lined baking sheet, and bake for 10–12 minutes or until they are fully dried out, a little crisp, and a shade darker than the rectangles. Leave to cool, then put in a food processor with the almonds and process into crumbs. Store in an airtight container until needed.

For the filling, put the crème fraîche, sugar, vanilla extract, lemon zest, and juice in a bowl and whisk until combined. Whip the cream to soft peaks, then use a large metal spoon to gently fold it into the crème fraîche mixture.

When you're ready to assemble the cake, line your 1 lb (450 g) loaf pan with plastic wrap. Generously spread one of the honey cookie layers with the filling and place, filling side up, in the base of the pan. Repeat until all the cake is used up—the cake will be higher than the sides of the pan, but that's okay.

Spread the remainder of the filling over the top and sides of the cake and then cover with crumbs, saving some for serving. Chill the cake in the fridge overnight—during this time, the moisture in the filling will soak into the layers and the flavors will develop.

For the mascarpone cream, beat the sugar into the mascarpone to incorporate. Whip the cream to stiff peaks, then gently fold into the mascarpone mixture, along with the lemon juice.

To serve, carefully lift the cake out of the pan and cut into 1-inch (2.5 cm) slices, then sprinkle with crumbs. Place a slice of cake on each plate and top with a dollop of the mascarpone cream.

In 1805, when Nelson won the Battle of Trafalgar, his ships were rigged with rope made from Latvian hemp, a miraculous plant we should be making more use of in the modern world; these crunchy cookies are a fun place to start.

If you can't get hold of unhulled hemp seeds, you can use the hulled variety. This will give your cookies a different consistency and a lighter hue, but they'll be just as delicious. With unhulled hemp seeds, I've found that I don't usually need much oil, if any; if you think it needs some, drizzle it in slowly and stop as soon as the hemp butter comes together.

HEMP BUTTER & WHITE CHOCOLATE COOKIES

MAKES 12–16

* Generous ½ cup (100 g) whole unhulled hemp seeds (see page 245)
* 1½ tablespoons hempseed oil
* 5 tablespoons (70 g) unsalted butter, at room temperature
* ½ cup, lightly packed (70 g) soft brown sugar
* 1 small egg, lightly beaten
* 1 teaspoon vanilla extract
* Generous ½ cup (70 g) all-purpose flour
* Generous 1 tablespoon cacao powder
* ½ teaspoon baking powder
* ½ teaspoon ground cinnamon
* ¼ teaspoon salt
* 1¾ oz (50 g) white chocolate, broken into small pieces

VEGETARIAN

Toast the hemp seeds in a dry frying pan over medium heat for about 7–8 minutes or until they smell nutty, stirring often. Tip the seeds into a powerful food processor and blend, scraping the sides down every so often, until you have a damp, powdery paste. Slowly pour in the oil and keep blending until it turns into one mass. (Alternatively, with such a small amount, you could pound the seeds using a mortar and pestle, then stir in the oil.) Set this hemp butter aside and rinse out the food processor.

In the food processor, beat together the butter and sugar until fluffy. With the machine running, add the egg and vanilla extract, followed by the hemp butter, and keep mixing until everything is well combined. (If you don't have a food processor, you can do this in a mixing bowl with a wooden spoon.)

Sift the flour into a large bowl with the cacao powder, baking powder, cinnamon, and salt.

Scrape the hemp butter mixture into the flour mixture and combine thoroughly to make a rather wet dough. Stir in the white chocolate, then chill in the fridge for 20 minutes, or overnight.

When you're ready to bake your cookies, preheat the oven to 350°F (180°C) and line a baking sheet with parchment paper.

Place teaspoonfuls of the dough on the baking sheet and gently press down on the top of each one with a fork. Bake the cookies for 14 minutes, then leave to cool on the pan for 2 minutes before transferring to a wire rack to cool completely.

At an ice-cream parlor in the small but elegant Latvian town of Cesis, I came across Gotina-flavored ice cream. When I asked what it was, the reply came that it was "a very Latvian thing," so naturally I had to order it, and quickly recognized the taste as that of the *krówki* (fudge) sweets of my childhood. Later we bought a packet of Gotina from a local shop and, sure enough, only the name was different—the cows on the wrappers, the rich, milky flavor, and the gooey texture were all identical to the Polish fudge I grew up with. This fudge makes a lovely gift, when cut into squares and individually wrapped; it will keep in the fridge for a couple of weeks.

HOMEMADE FUDGE
WITH POPPYSEEDS

SERVES 12–20, depending on size of pieces

* 1 x 14 oz (400 g) can of condensed milk
* Generous 1 tablespoon poppyseeds
* Pinch of salt
* 3½ tablespoons (50 g) unsalted butter

VEGETARIAN

Line a small baking pan or ovenproof dish with parchment paper—I use a glass baking dish about 12 inches x 8 inches (30 cm x 20 cm).

Pour the condensed milk into a frying pan and place over medium heat. Once the color starts changing to a light golden, add the poppyseeds and salt. Keep heating, stirring constantly, for another 15 minutes or until it turns golden brown.

Finally, add the butter and stir until melted, then take off the heat, and carefully pour into the baking pan or dish.

Leave to cool, then cut the fudge into squares or rectangles and chill in the fridge for about 30 minutes. Remember to take it out about 10 minutes before you want to eat it!

VILNIUS:

WHERE TWO RIVERS MEET

The specific place my exiled Grandma Halinka longed for was "Wilno" (the Polish name for Vilnius), where she had grown up. Having always hoped to visit, I had expected to feel some kind of affinity with the city when I finally got there, but I did not expect to fall in love at first sight. Its staggering beauty charmed me from the outset.

Vilnius, the capital of Lithuania, lies at the confluence of two rivers: the meandering Vilnia, from which the city takes its name; and the fast-flowing Neris. When I was a child, my grandma had told me about a river where she swam on hot days, and although our rental car should have been returned an hour earlier, it was such a hot day that I couldn't resist a dip in the Neris first. And of course I was further enticed by the romantic notion of swimming in the same river my grandmother had swum in as a girl. On that sweltering day, the river had a current so strong it would have swept me away if I had stopped paddling for even a moment, but there was a sandy beach on one side and a steep, lush bank on the other, making the

Neris feel like it was in the middle of nowhere, rather than so close to a city.

I found the city's food scene just as appealing. On top of a steep hill sits the Hales Turgus, a lovingly renovated market hall dating from 1906. Nestled among the fruit and vegetable stalls are cozy eateries and exquisite delicatessens, including my favorite shop in Vilnius, Roots, where you can try Lithuanian cheeses to rival France's finest, traditional sourdough bread, cold-pressed oils, and thoughtfully crafted local wines.

At the chic and sophisticated Džiausgmas restaurant, I let myself be inspired by the wave of creativity that swept across our table, while Nusia contentedly picked cherry tomatoes that were ripening in the sunshine on the restaurant's terrace—the waiter said his son had the exact same idea! There was a sampler of home-cured meats and ferments, followed by chanterelles and blueberries fried in lard (reimagined as a vegetarian dish on page 146), zucchini flowers stuffed with zander in a creamy curry sauce, smoked carp with a fermented bean mayonnaise, rabbit

The city speaks softly of simple and noble things,
and does not open up for everyone.

JAN BUŁHAK, PHOTOGRAPHER, CIRCA 1939

*In Vilnius, a place with verdant riverbanks at its heart,
I fell in love with the bohemian cafes and bars, Baroque
architecture, intriguing murals, and outstanding local food.*

*A sweep of terracotta rooftops in Vilnius's Old Town
is dominated by the white facade and distinctive red spire
of the Evangelical Lutheran Church.*

fritters, and an ornate raspberry and tomato salad. It felt as if each ingredient had been affectionately tended and carefully prepared, and the whole experience was unforgettable.

✖

There's an open-heartedness to Vilnius, which can be traced right back to the city's birth, when those of all religions were invited to come and put down roots, provided they respect local pagan traditions and remained loyal to its ruler (only the Teutonic Knights were excluded, detested as they were for their controlling brutality). Over the centuries, people of many ethnicities and cultures settled here, and Vilnius became known as a diverse, vital, and artistic place, while still retaining

a village-like feel. With its towering trees and quaint duck ponds, interrupted by monumental Baroque architecture, the city has nurtured this atmosphere to this day.

According to local lore, Vilnius was founded when, after a day spent hunting in a sacred forest, Grand Duke Gediminas had a dream of a howling iron wolf, which his chief priest interpreted as a harbinger of fame and prosperity should he establish a city on that site. Gediminas duly built a castle on a hill at the confluence of the two rivers, and Vilnius became the capital of the Grand Duchy of Lithuania. The city first entered written history in 1323, when the pope received a letter from Gediminas, expressing his wish to convert to Christianity.

Although he wanted to put Vilnius on the map of Europe, Gediminas's resolve faltered as his baptism approached, and he declared that his letter had been either misunderstood or miswritten. In the end, Lithuania only converted to Catholicism after the marriage of Gediminas's grandson Jagiełło to the Polish queen Jadwiga in 1386.

Following the establishment of the Polish-Lithuanian Commonwealth in 1569, the capital moved to the Polish city of Kraków, and then to Warsaw, yet Vilnius continued to thrive. Centuries of peace and tolerance ended, however, with the Russian invasion of the city in 1655, and by 1795, Vilnius was entirely under Russian control. The still-flourishing Vilnius University was closed in 1832 after a failed Polish-Lithuanian revolt, and the Lithuanian language was banned not long afterwards. The Industrial Revolution came late to Vilnius, but brought some hope: investment started flowing into the city again, and living conditions improved. With businesses growing, so did the population, and soon Lithuanians began to mobilize. However, the onset of World War I brought instability and over the following years Vilnius came under foreign control many times. During the Nazi occupation, the Jewish population was decimated, traumatizing the city for generations to come, and Soviet annexation in 1940 and 1944 brought mass deportations, instilling fear and paranoia in the inhabitants for more than fifty years, before independence saw Vilnius resume its place as capital of Lithuania.

While Lithuania officially broke away from Moscow in 1990, it was not an easy separation, and on 13th January 1991 the city of Vilnius was in the news worldwide, with "Bloodshed at Lithuanian TV station" making the headlines. As the people of Vilnius stood, unarmed, to protect city buildings from a Russian takeover, the last words uttered on air before the station was forced to shut down were: "We address all those who hear us. It is possible that [the army] can break us with force or close our mouths, but no one will make us renounce freedom and independence." The fight for a free Lithuania was won that day, though not without casualties—fourteen civilians were killed, and more than 700 seriously injured. The rest of the decade was a wild and lawless time in all of the newly independent countries across the region, but by 1997 a conscious decision was made to start rebuilding Vilnius. The crumbling Old Town (now listed as a UNESCO World Heritage site), which had been painfully neglected during Soviet rule, would be renovated and reclaimed.

In her short-story collection *Vilnius, Wilno, Wilna*, Lithuanian writer Kristina Sabaliauskaitė traces the changing fortunes of the city through the voices of three erstwhile residents of the city: a Polish girl, Jadwiga; a Jewish businessman who escaped the Nazis and made his fortune in New York; and an old-school Lithuanian Communist. "Franco's Black Pearls," set in the interwar years, portrays the loss of Jadwiga's youthful innocence as strange and terrible events unfold around her.

My Grandma Halinka would have been about the same age as Jadwiga, and was still living in Vilnius at that time. So, for me, seeing the city through Jadwiga's eyes was like reliving my grandmother's youth. She went back to Vilnius only once, during the mid-1990s, but was so broken-hearted to see her childhood home looking run down and shell shocked that she never returned again. I fondly imagine that my grandmother saw the city anew through my eyes last summer. Like a risen phoenix, its former glory was visible in every elegant Baroque building; its streets were alive with music; its cafes full of stylish bohemian youth. Finally, the spirit of Vilnius has triumphed.

Ending my trip in Vilnius felt like coming full circle. The match ignited by the stories of Vilnius I had been told in childhood had grown into a bigger flame that lit my way across the Baltic States, ultimately bringing me to the streets of the city my grandma left behind all those years ago, though they never truly left her.

✖

A balmy afternoon in Vilnius's trendy Užupis district, presided over by the bronze angel sculpture that has come to symbolize the area's independent spirit.

DRINKS

Without a doubt, the non-alcoholic drinks that are most common across the Baltics are *kvass*, kefir, and birch water. Unfortunately, birch water does not keep for long, perhaps a couple of days, so it's something to add to your list if you decide to travel to the Baltics. Fermented grain-based *kvass* and milk kefir, however, are now among my favorite soft drinks.

The spritzers and cocktails in this chapter are either inspired by Baltic ingredients or loosely based on drinks I tried during my travels in the region. In Estonia, wine is traditionally made from fruit other than grapes—sparkly rhubarb wine was my favorite—and so I have developed some zesty fruit-based drinks to reflect that aspect of the culture.

Kvass comes in as many hues as amber: it can be cloudy or clear, malty and dark like cola, or so light and zingy that it resembles lemon sherbet. The recipe is inspired by a waitress at a Riga restaurant who gave us some of her homemade *kvass*, even though it wasn't on the menu. She had developed the recipe in order to reduce food waste at the restaurant. Its pale color and citrusy taste made it stand out (most of the *kvass* we had been drinking on the trip was dark brown and malty) and it was wonderfully refreshing. The waitress insisted that the seeds in the bread gave her *kvass* a special something, so I suggest you use seeded rye bread or throw a handful of toasted sunflower seeds in with the bread and citrus zests before pouring in the water. *Kvass* makes a great alternative to beer and is thought to be very good for you; I would love it if it became more popular, just as kombucha has in recent years.

LEMON & ORANGE KVASS

MAKES a 6-cup (1.5-liter) bottle

- 10½ oz (300 g) stale dark rye bread, cut into chunks
- Zest of 1 unwaxed lemon, in strips
- Zest of 1 unwaxed orange, in strips
- Generous ¾ cup (200 ml) runny honey
- Generous 1 tablespoon sourdough starter (see page 64)
- 6 cups (1.5 liters) water

VEGETARIAN

Preheat the oven to 400°F (200°C). Scatter the bread over a baking sheet and toast in the oven for about 15 minutes, adding the lemon and orange zest for the final 5 minutes. The bread should be browned but not burnt.

Transfer the bread and zest to a large bowl or jar, then add the honey and sourdough starter. Pour in the water and stir well with a wooden spoon (metal utensils can interfere with the fermentation process). Cover with a clean tea towel and leave at room temperature for 3–4 days, stirring it with a wooden spoon once a day.

When the *kvass* is ready, strain it twice through a cheesecloth-lined sieve, then leave to settle overnight and strain once more.

To sterilize your bottle, first put it through a hot dishwasher cycle or hand-wash in hot, soapy water. Then submerge it in vigorously boiling water for 10 minutes, pour out the water, and allow to air-dry. Pour the *kvass* into the bottle, making sure it is no more than three-quarters full, then seal.

Store your *kvass* in the fridge or somewhere cold to ferment slowly for about a week, releasing the lid once a day to "burp" it and release any fermentation gases. Drink within two weeks.

A NOTE ON EXPLODING BOTTLES

Remember to burp your *kvass* and keep it out of harm's way. If you burp the bottle once a day, it won't explode, but if you forget (so easy to do …) it just might, especially if your bottle is airtight and your kitchen is warm. After a couple of bad experiences with exploding bottles, I now use fermentation-grade bottles for my *kvass* and leave it out in the shed until I am ready to drink it. Best to play it safe!

Estonians will often stir *kama*—usually a mixture of ground wheat, rye, barley, and peas—into a glass of kefir, then either sweeten it or add salt to taste. It makes a quick, nutritious snack or speedy breakfast. The *kama* here is enriched with flaxseed and peas; if you prefer a plainer, more basic *kama*, there's a simple version on page 36.

Although flaxseed is not usually found in *kama*, sixteenth-century Estonia was known as the "house of wax and flax," so I add it here without compunction. A friend who grew up in Japan told me that *kama* reminded her of the Japanese roasted soybean flour called *kinako*—another much less authentic, but delicious, ingredient that I sometimes add to the mix.

KAMA KEFIR

SERVES 2

* 1 teaspoon birch syrup (see page 245) or maple syrup
* 2 cups (500 ml) milk kefir

For the kama
* ½ cup (50 g) dried green peas
* ½ cup (50 g) rolled oats
* ½ cup (50 g) barley flakes
* ½ cup (50 g) rye flakes
* 5 tablespoons ground flaxseed (linseed)
* Salt

VEGETARIAN

For the *kama*, place the peas in one bowl, and the rolled oats, barley, and rye flakes in another. Pour enough water into each bowl to cover the contents by about ¾ inch (2 cm), then leave to soak for 2 hours.

Preheat the oven to 400°F (200°C) and ready two baking sheets.

Drain the soaked peas and cook them in a saucepan of boiling salted water for 30 minutes, then drain thoroughly again.

Spread out the peas on one baking sheet. Drain the soaked oats, barley, and rye flakes and spread out on the other baking sheet.

Roast the peas and grains for 40 minutes, then leave to cool.

Tip the cooled peas and grains into a food processor and grind to a coarse flour consistency. Transfer the *kama* to a bowl and stir in the flaxseed.

Place a heaped tablespoon of *kama* and a teaspoon of birch or maple syrup in each glass, then pour in the kefir, mix thoroughly, and drink. (The rest of the *kama* will keep for at least a month in an airtight container, and is great sprinkled over yogurt, muesli, or ice cream.)

Kefir, the drink of my childhood in Poland, is loved just as much by the people of the Baltics. Fortunately, it is now increasingly available, either plain or sweetened, and I like to use it as a base for a fruit smoothie, such as this invigorating berry one (photographed on page 34).

KEFIR BERRY SMOOTHIE

SERVES 2

* 1 teaspoon unsweetened dried cranberries (ideally with no added juice or oils)
* 1⅔ cups (400 ml) milk kefir
* Scant ½ cup (50 g) raspberries
* Generous 1 tablespoon birch syrup (see page 245) or maple syrup
* Couple of ice cubes
* 2 large or 4 small strawberries

VEGETARIAN

Finely grind the cranberries in a powerful food processor or blender. Add the kefir, raspberries, birch or maple syrup, and ice cubes and mix to a smooth, pale pink shake.

Add the strawberries and pulse a few times, so you still have some fruity strawberry bits in your smoothie, then pour into glasses to serve.

In the Baltics, the plump bright orange berries of sea buckthorn are everywhere in the summer months. This sea buckthorn lemonade is simple to make and so refreshing—the sharp, sour taste of the berries really comes through. If you're feeling frisky, top it up with prosecco instead of sparkling water.

SEA BUCKTHORN LEMONADE

SERVES 4

* 1 unwaxed lemon
* ⅓ cup (50 g) sea buckthorn berries (see page 246)
* ½ cup (100 g) sugar
* 1⅔ cups (400 ml) chilled water
* Generous ¾ cup (200 ml) sparkling water

VEGAN

Cut the (unpeeled) lemon into chunks and remove the seeds.

Place the lemon chunks, sea buckthorn berries, sugar, and chilled water into a food processor and blend to a pulp. Pass through a sieve into a jug, pressing down with the back of a spoon to extract as much liquid as possible.

Top up with sparkling water, then stir well and pour into glasses.

The "quince" grown in the Baltic States is actually chaenomeles fruit, also known as Japanese quince. Sadly this hard, sour fruit is not easy to find in shops but I happen to have some growing in my garden, so I decided to include this Baltic-style bellini, in case you do too (or you could use crab apples instead). The recipe is dedicated to my friend Linda, who took great pains to explain the ins and outs of Latvian food to me—including the widespread misconception about Baltic "quince." *Prieka*, Linda!

BALTIC BELLINI

SERVES 2

* 4–5 chaenomeles fruit
  (or 10 crab apples),
  cut in half
* 2½ tablespoons sugar
* Generous 1 tablespoon honey
* ½ teaspoon vanilla extract
* Dash of Angostura bitters—
  optional
* Generous ¾ cup (200 ml)
  chilled prosecco

VEGETARIAN

Put the fruit into a small saucepan with the sugar, honey, and a generous ¾ cup (200 ml) of water—or 1⅔ cups (400 ml) if using crab apples. Bring to a boil, then simmer for 10 minutes, or until the fruit has turned to mush (for crab apples this will take closer to 30 minutes). Stir in the vanilla extract and leave to cool.

Pass the fruit mush through a sieve into a bowl, pressing down with the back of a spoon to extract as much puree as possible.

Place a teaspoon of the fruit puree in the bottom of two champagne flutes or other glasses. Add a few drops of bitters, if using, then pour in a little of the prosecco and stir.

Top up with the rest of the prosecco, stir once more, then serve.

I love everything about this martini. With its heady fragrance, subtle sharpness, and amber hue, it's perfect for a girls' night in.

RHUBARB VODKA MARTINI

SERVES 2

* 2 rhubarb stalks, trimmed and
  cut into 3-inch (8 cm) lengths
* Generous 1 tablespoon sugar
* 1 teaspoon vanilla extract
* 1 teaspoon rosewater
* Scant ½ cup (100 ml) vodka
* Handful of ice cubes
* Dash of Angostura bitters

VEGETARIAN

Put the rhubarb into a stainless steel saucepan with the sugar and ⅔ cup (150 ml) of water. Bring to a boil, then turn the heat down to a simmer and cook until the rhubarb has fallen apart, about 15 minutes. Stir in the vanilla extract and rosewater.

Press the stewed rhubarb through a sieve into a bowl, pressing down with the back of a spoon to extract as much puree as possible. Leave the puree to cool, then chill in the fridge.

Spoon the rhubarb puree into a cocktail shaker, add the vodka, ice, and a couple of drops of bitters and shake vigorously (if you don't have a cocktail shaker, you can just muddle everything together in a jug). Strain into two martini or other glasses.

Fruit wines are very popular in Estonia, and I particularly liked a blackberry one I had at a "house cafe" during my travels. The hospitable Estonians seem to love turning their homes into pop-up cafes where they can showcase their local food and drinks, and since trying new food and drinks is my favorite pastime, I enjoyed the tradition immensely. This fruity spritzer captures the essence of that blackberry wine, without having to go to the trouble of winemaking at home—which feels like a step too far, even for me!

BLACKBERRY WINE SPRITZER

SERVES 2

* ⅔ cup (100 g) blackberries
* 1¼ cups (300 ml) chilled white wine
* Generous ¾ cup (200 ml) chilled soda water

VEGAN

Crush the blackberries to a puree using a mortar and pestle or blender. Spoon the puree into a jug, pour in the white wine, and stir well to combine.

Pass the contents of the jug through a fine-meshed or cheesecloth-lined sieve to remove the seeds, then pour into two glasses and top up with soda water.

This is a very seasonal cocktail, because you need to gather the elderflowers when they are at their peak—white and fluffy, without any discoloration—in late spring. If you don't have access to an elderberry plant, you could use store-bought elderflower syrup instead, but the homemade stuff tastes wonderful.

ELDERFLOWER & VODKA SPRITZER

SERVES 2

* 3 tablespoons vodka
* 1¼ cups (300 ml) chilled soda water
* 4 sprigs of mint
* Handful of ice cubes

For the elderflower syrup

* 10–12 heads of elderflower, well washed
* 2⅔ cups (500 g) sugar
* Zest of 1 unwaxed lemon, in strips
* 4¼ cups (1 liter) filtered or bottled water

VEGAN

For the elderflower syrup, put the elderflower heads into a stainless steel pot with the sugar, lemon zest, and water. Bring to a boil, stirring until the sugar dissolves, then turn down the heat and simmer for 15 minutes.

Strain through a sieve into a jug, pressing down with the back of a spoon to extract as much syrup as possible. Discard the elderflowers. Transfer the syrup to a sterilized 1-quart (1-liter) bottle (see page 174); it will keep for at least a month in the fridge.

To make the spritzer, pour 3 tablespoons of the syrup into a clean jug, then add the vodka, soda water, and half of the mint. Stir to combine, then serve over ice, with a sprig of mint in each glass.

A NOTE ON VODKA

Any good-quality vodka works well in this, but if you fancy a change, try making it with Polish *Żubrówka* bison-grass vodka for a herbal note that beautifully complements the elderflower.

Echoes of pagan lore ... reed sculpture at Amber Bay, on the Curonian Spit in Lithuania.

THE AMBER TRAIL

Throughout history, the "gold of the north" has been treasured as a sacred amulet or noble ornament, a medicine, and a source of economic power. Created some 40–60 million years ago from the sap of prehistoric conifer trees, this captivating resin is found in abundance in the Baltic Sea.

When we describe something as "amber," we are usually thinking of a translucent orange color, but amber comes in a range of hues from a pale lemon-sherbet yellow to a dark chocolate brown. Walking along a Baltic beach after a storm might reveal tiny little pebbles of amber in the sand, light as plastic and rather cloudy. Only when polished does the resin take on the radiant, nitid appearance it is famed for. Yet, polished or not, there's a warmth to amber—it is pleasant to the touch, and a nugget of amber seems to respond to human skin, growing warm when held in the palm of the hand.

From the earliest days of human civilization, this fossilized resin has found its way from the Baltic region southwards along the so-called Amber Trail. Like most trading routes, this wasn't one specific road, but rather a network of routes, political and economic ties spanning thousands of years. However, if we were to look at a map of Europe together, I could draw you a rough outline of the path traveled by the amber merchants. Starting in the southeastern Baltic Sea, on the coastline of Estonia (although amber is rarely found here now, it may once have been a source), Latvia, and Lithuania, we would pass through the modern-day Russian outpost of Kaliningrad before heading along Poland's Vistula River and onwards to Greece and Rome.

Amber has held us fascinated through the ages. In prehistoric times, the golden resin was used by local tribes for sacred rites and healing, possibly linked to its electrostatic properties. According to amber art expert Dr Anna Sobecka, animal figurines thought to date from the Mesolithic were used as talismans, either to offer protection to their owners or to ensure success in hunting the animals represented, and by the Neolithic Age, round amber amulets with a hole in the middle featured in sun worship. The further south amber went, the more its rarity and exotic appearance made it a sought-after status symbol. Relics found at burial sites in Egypt (including the tomb of Tutankhamun) and the Near East suggest that the amber trade was well established in ancient times.

In Greek antiquity, the creation of amber was enshrined in Greek mythology. Phaethon ("the radiant") was the son of Helios the sun god and water nymph Clymene; however, Helios could not stay with his family as he had to take the sun across the sky each day from east to west. Helios's absence led Phaethon to test his father and, seeking answers, he traveled to the sun god's luminous castle in India. Touched by the boy's plight, Helios granted him one wish. Phaethon asked to drive the chariot of the sun for one day— and, having made a pledge, Helios could not refuse.

On the fiery journey, the horses reacted to Phaeton's inexperience and steered him into danger, creating a gash in the sky, which became the Milky Way; the sun also veered dangerously close to the earth, burning the continent of Africa. Witnessing the destruction, Zeus struck down Phaethon and his body fell into a river. Phaeton's seven sisters, the Heliades, cried for their brother and were turned into poplar trees, destined to grow by the river and guard his body for ever more; their shed tears turned to amber. Clearly, the ancient Greeks were aware that the "tears" (sap) of trees hardens into a resin. Like the prehistoric peoples before them, they also recognized amber's connection with energy, naming it *elektron*, from which the English word electricity is derived.

Eventually, amber fell out of favor in Greece. However, amber jewelry and figurines made by the Etruscans suggest the trail must have persisted, and demand for amber rose again during Roman times, when it was prized for its unusual color. The ladies of the Roman elite were particularly fond of it, and in a status-obsessed society, one way for a Roman gentleman to impress his fellow citizens was to throw a wild party, using vast amounts of amber to decorate everything. Amber powder was also taken as medicine and carried as a cooling perfume in the hot, Mediterranean sun. And so this humble resin found on the beaches of the Baltic Sea became one of five components that were essential to the Roman economy, along with pepper, frankincense, ivory, and myrrh. The Amber Trail duly expanded and there is evidence of another route across the Black Sea, in addition to the Vistula River route.

Around 98 AD, Roman historian Tacitus noted that the Aesti people of the Baltic region were the only ones to " ... collect amber—*glaesum* is their own word for it—in the shallows or even on the beach." So it is perhaps unsurprising that Lithuanian folk legends wove a romantic thread into the story of Baltic amber. The goddess of the seas, Jurate, lived in an otherworldly amber palace at the bottom of the Baltic Sea. One day, Jurate decided to punish a young fisherman, Kastytis, who had been plundering the sea of fish. However, when she saw the dashing young fisherman, she immediately fell in love and took him back to her amber kingdom. And there they lived peacefully until Perkunas, god of thunder and guardian of morality and the divine order, learned of their affair— a mortal and a god were not permitted to be together. Angered, Perkunas struck Jurate's underwater palace with a thunderbolt, killing Kastytis. In some versions of this tale the nuggets of amber washing up on Baltic shores are the tears of the sea goddess crying over her dead lover; in others, they are the remains of her amber palace.

As life ebbed and flowed, so did the demand for amber, and with the fall of the Roman Empire, it declined once more. The trail itself survived, however, since northern Italy remained rich enough to continue buying amber and, in time, Constantinople took over from Rome as the new destination for Baltic amber. Meanwhile, a new religion was taking hold of Europe, one described by Pliny the Younger (nephew of Pliny the Elder) as "depraved, excessive superstition." As Christianity grew, so did the demand for amber rosary beads. Around the thirteenth century, the Teutonic Knights took over the territories of Prussia, declaring themselves the sole owners of all Baltic amber and introducing harsh punishments for anyone found collecting it. Raw amber, the source of their economic power, was guarded in a treasury.

Change only came when the Protestant reformation took hold and rosaries fell out of favor. With amber's fortunes waning, the Teutonic Knights surrendered control of the amber trade to the Koehn von Jaski family of merchants from Gdańsk, who found a market for amber in the Middle East. Sensing another shift, Prussia again took over the amber trade—and, yet again, protecting their monopoly cost them more money than it made them. Cutting their losses, they sold amber-mining rights to the highest bidder, Stantien and Becker. Predictably enough, when the company made a successful business out of it, the Prussian government took over once more; however, amber production was badly impacted by two World Wars and never quite recovered.

The journey of amber has come full circle. Across the Baltic region, the resin is once again appreciated for its aesthetic beauty, and for the health and protective properties it is believed to hold. Its honeyed hues adorn jewelry shops, where its authenticity is demonstrated in salt water (real amber floats). If you're lucky, you might still find amber pebbles on a Baltic beach after a stormy night, but economies are no longer built upon it.

✖

The ancient network known as the Amber Trail—or Amber Road—connected the Baltics to the rest of Europe, and I think it's reasonable to assume that it wasn't only amber that traveled along these trade routes. The same people who sought amber most likely shared stories, ideas, food and spices, and probably recipes too.

During my own Baltic odyssey I often found myself reflecting on the power of amber. During childhood vacations on the Polish Baltic coast, I remember finding tiny nuggets in the powdery sand beneath my feet. Rubbing the resin in my hand, I would immediately feel as if I'd found something special. I visualized the first people to roam these endless beaches finding amber and discovering its properties through their senses, unmediated by science. In my mind's eye, I could see them carving the resin into magical totems and figurines. I pondered what machinery the ancient Romans would have used to unearth huge amounts of amber

for their lavish parties. I imagined the curious Greeks discovering that amber could create sparks of electricity when rubbed on wool. I felt the excitement of scientists who continue to find fossilized insects captured inside amber, sometimes frozen in the act of moving or laying eggs.

The human fascination with amber is multi-faceted, but for me it's the idea that such an expanse of time is encapsulated in one little nugget. If only amber could talk, the stories it would tell …

✖

INGREDIENTS & STOCKISTS

Here you will find more detailed information on ingredients used in this book and where you can find them. As I am Polish, and there are many Polish shops in the UK, I tend to recommend trying them first—partly out of convenience, and partly because I know they will stock the majority of items needed—but I imagine other Eastern European food stores would also have the same things or an equivalent. Note that although you can often buy many of these ingredients from the "world foods" section of larger supermarkets, their range and stock levels can be erratic.

AQUAFABA

While this isn't a specifically Baltic ingredient, it is used in vegan cooking as a substitute for egg and egg white, and it features in some of the vegan recipes I have developed for the book. Aquafaba is simply the cooking liquid from chickpeas, either home-cooked or canned. Because there are concerns about some of the substances used to line cans, I recommend making your own aquafaba by soaking ⅓ cup (70 g) dried chickpeas in 1¼ cups (300 ml) water overnight, then simmering them in that water until tender. (The cooked chickpeas will keep for a few days in the fridge or several months in the freezer, and can be used to make the wild garlic hummus on page 67 or the salad on page 156.)

BARLEY

The world's largest producer of barley is Russia, so perhaps it's no coincidence that this grain is very popular in the Baltic States. In Polish shops, you can buy both pearl barley, called *pęczak*, and pot barley or barley groats, confusingly called *kasza jęczmienna*; note that these are not interchangeable, so you'll need to check the kind needed for your recipe. You can often find barley in health food stores and the "whole foods" section of some supermarkets.

BIRCH SYRUP

Birch syrup is the Estonian answer to maple syrup—and although the flavor differs, you can use the two interchangeably. Estonian birch syrup can be bought direct from Kasekunst, at birchsyrup.eu, but birch syrup is also produced in North America, and is available at alaskabirchsyrup.com and georgiamountainmaples.com.

BUCKWHEAT

Found all over Eastern Europe, buckwheat is a staple ingredient in the Baltic countries and Russia. A particular favorite is roasted buckwheat, which looks like raw buckwheat except that it is dark brown in color. It has a distinctive nutty flavor and can be found in any Polish shop—look for *kasza gryczana prażona* on the package—and most health food stores, where it may be called kasha.

Buckwheat, whether raw or roasted, is cooked like rice, using the absorption method on the hob: allow about ½ inch (1 cm) of water above the buckwheat, then let it simmer and steam, covered, over very low heat, for about 20 minutes or until all the water has been absorbed. I always wrap the pan of cooked buckwheat, lid and all, in a towel or tea towel and then cover it with a blanket to keep the grains warm and fluffy, just like my gran (and many other Eastern European grans) would.

PICKLES IN BRINE

These small cucumbers preserved in brine taste quite different to the ones pickled in vinegar, and you can also use the brine to add flavor to soups and dressings. They are available at any Polish shop (called *ogórki kwaszone* or *ogórki kiszone*) and in the "world foods" section of most supermarkets.

HEMP SEEDS, OIL & BUTTER

I could rave about the brilliance of the hemp plant, its many benefits, and how shamefully under-used it is. Hemp butter is a traditional Latvian spread made from hemp seeds and their oil, and it has been enjoying something of a renaissance in recent years.

If you want to make it at home (see page 18), you should be able to find unhulled hemp seeds and hempseed oil at health food stores or online. Note, however, that unhulled hemp seeds are impossible to get hold of, or even illegal, in some countries—in which case, you can replace them with the hulled variety.

LATVIAN GREEN CHEESE

A truly unique product with an irreplaceable umami flavor, this dried curd cheese from Latvia is infused with blue fenugreek. It lifts any dish, but I especially like it on pasta and salads. It is produced by the Ceriņi family: you can see their range at sierarazotne.lv and email them your order at sierarazotne@gmail.com; and if you go to Latvia you can even visit the factory.

To make your own approximation, take 1 cup (100 g) of finely grated mature hard cheese, such as aged pecorino or parmesan, and spread it out on a baking sheet lined with parchment paper. Place in a 150°F (70°C) oven to dry for 20 minutes, then mix 2 teaspoons of ground blue fenugreek (available from herb and spice suppliers) into the dried cheese and return to the oven for 5 minutes, or until its pungent aroma fills your kitchen. Turn off the oven and allow the cheese to cool inside for about 20 minutes or so before grinding to a fine powder. It will keep in an airtight container in the fridge for a couple of weeks.

MAYONNAISE

When most people think of an Eastern European "salad," they tend to imagine something covered in mayonnaise. Although the Baltic States have moved away from this older style of cooking somewhat, mayonnaise remains popular. Of course you can buy good-quality mayonnaise, but I find the best way to elevate a dish is to make your own (see page 58—just leave out the chives).

POPPYSEEDS

Poppyseeds are used with abandon in Baltic cooking. Given the quantities involved, I recommend buying them from a Polish or Eastern European delicatessen.

RAPESEED OIL

I like to have two oils on hand: an ordinary one (such as the Polish *Kujawski* brand) for deep-frying; and a good-quality cold-pressed one for shallow-frying and everything else. You should be able to find rapeseed oil in most supermarkets and all Polish shops. Substitute canola.

RED RYE MALT POWDER

Made from roasted barley malt, this ingredient is useful when it comes to reproducing the distinctive taste of the malty dark breads I ate in the Baltics, since it seems that the flours you can get there aren't always available here. Find it online.

RYE FLOUR

Rye bread is the most popular bread in the Baltics, due to the grain growing so well on Baltic soil. In each country it tastes slightly different, though; Estonia, for instance, has its own special black bread called *leib*. I always use wholemeal rye flour for my bread; you can buy it from supermarkets these days.

SAUERKRAUT

This fermented cabbage is very popular across Eastern Europe and in Germany too, so you should have no trouble finding it in any Polish, Ukrainian, or German food shop, as well as many supermarkets—just make sure you get the most natural one possible, without any artificial additives. All the same, I would encourage you to make it yourself—it's very simple and you just can't beat the taste of the homemade stuff (see page 176).

SEA BUCKTHORN BERRIES

In the Baltic States, you can buy a large container of these vivid orange berries for a euro. Although sea buckthorn also grows in the UK and North America, it is much harder to come by. Frozen or dried sea buckthorn berries can be bought online and in health food shops; soak dried berries in apple juice for an hour before using. If you have no luck with sourcing any of these, you could substitute fresh cranberries in savory dishes, and raspberries in sweet dishes.

SUGAR

I like to use raw and less refined sugars, such as organic cane sugar or light muscovado sugar, in my cooking, since I prefer the taste.

TWARÓG

This Eastern European fresh soft cheese can be bought from Polish shops and some supermarkets—I always go for the full-fat kind, labeled *Twaróg tłusty*. You could use any other curd cheese, such as farmer cheese or ricotta, instead.

WILD GARLIC

I came across wild garlic (ramsons) in many forms in the Baltics, and it grows in abundance in cool, shady woodlands across Europe. In North America, its closest relative is ramps. You can sometimes find these fresh in farmers' markets in spring (look for ramp leaves harvested without the bulbs—harvesting the entire plant, rather than just the leaves, has weakened the wild plant population of late). Fermented wild garlic can sometimes be found in Russian or Eastern European markets or online (sometimes labeled pickled wild garlic).

SOURCES

Epp Annus, Piret Peiker & Liina Lukas, 2013, "Colonial Regimes in the Baltic States," *Interlitteraria*, 18 (2), 545–554

Hilary Bird (editor and translator), 2018, *An Introduction to Estonian Literature*, Slavica, Bloomington, Indiana

Audrone Bliujiene, 2011, *Northern Gold: Amber in Lithaunia (c. 100 to c. 1200)*, Brill, Leiden

Laimonas Briedis, 2008, *Vilnius—City of Strangers*, Vilnius: Baltos lankos, Vilnius

Eva Eglaja-Kriststone & Becca Parkinson (editors), 2018, *The Book of Riga: A City in Short Fiction*, Comma Press, Manchester

Mindaugas Grikpėdis & Giedrė Motuzaitė Matuzevičiūtė, 2016, "The beginnings of rye (*Secale cereale*) cultivation in the Baltics," *Vegetation History and Archaeobotany*, 25 (6), 601–610

Nora Ikstena, 2018, *Soviet Milk* (translated by Hilary Margita Gailitis), Pereine Press, London

Friedrich Reinhold Kreutzwald, 2011, *Kalevipoeg: The Estonian National Epic* (translated by Triinu Kartus), Estonian Literary Museum, Tartu

Willy Ley, 1951, *Dragons in Amber: Further Adventures of a Romantic Naturalist*, Viking Press, New York

Martin Lings, 1969, "Old Lithuanian Songs," *Studies in Comparative Religion*, 3 (1), Winter 1969

Diane Mincyte & Ulrike Plath (editors), 2017, *Food Culture and Politics in the Baltic States*, Routledge, Abingdon

Nils Muiznieks, Juris Rozenvalds & Ieva Birka, 2013, "Ethnicity and social cohesion in the post-Soviet Baltic states," *Patterns of Prejudice*, 47 (3), 288–308

Mihkel Mutt, 2015, *The Cavemen Chronicle* (translated by Adam Cullen), Dalkey Archive Press, Champaign, Illinois

Kevin O'Connor, 2003, *The History of the Baltic States*, Greenwood Press, Westport, Connecticut

Charles River Editors, 2019, *The Amber Road: The History and Legacy of the Ancient Trade Network that Moved Amber across Europe*, Charles River Editors audiobooks

Frederick William Rudler, 1911, "Amber," in Hugh Chisholm (editor), *Encyclopædia Britannica* (11th edition), Cambridge University Press, Cambridge

Kristina Sabaliauskaitė, 2015, *Vilnius. Wilno. Vilna. Three Short Stories* (translated by Romas Kinka), Baltos lankos, Vilnius

Antanas Škėma, 2018, *White Shroud* (translated by Karla Gruodis), Vagabond Voices, Glasgow

Guntis Šmidchens, 1996, *A Baltic Music: The Folklore Movement in Lithuania, Latvia and Estonia, 1968–1991*, Indiana University (electronic dissertation)

Tomas Tranströmer, 2015, *Bright Scythe: Selected Poems* (translated by Patty Crane), Sarabande Books, Louisville, Kentucky

Tomas Venclova, 2009, *Vilnius: A Personal History*, Sheep Meadow Press, New York

Jayde Will (editor), 2018, *New Baltic Poetry*, Parthian Books, Cardigan

Augustinas Žemaitis, truelithuania.com

ACKNOWLEDGMENTS

It takes many people to create a beautiful book. First of all, I would like to thank the publishing team: Corinne Roberts, for her belief and ongoing support; Vivien Valk and Justin Wolfers, for making *Amber & Rye* look and feel so special; and Alison Cowan, for editing it so thoughtfully and thoroughly. Thank you also to the Murdoch Books UK office, and especially to Jemma Crocker, for her invaluable input and marketing efforts.

A massive thanks to my lovely agent, Isabel Atherton, for being open to my ideas and always having my best interests at heart.

A big thank you goes to the photography dream team, who created the stunning food images for the book: photographer Ola O. Smit, for her passion and talent; Anna Wilkins, for such gorgeous props and styling; and Samantha Dixon, you are a star—thank you for making the shoot so easy and smooth. Thank you also to Kylee Newton, who came to help out—the day was made all the lovelier by your presence. Above all, thanks to everyone for making the experience so much fun.

In the field, thank you to my partner, Yasin Salazar, who did the travel photography in between looking after a three-year-old and driving around the entire Baltic States. We did it!

Across the Baltics, there are so many thank yous to be said—since my trip was only loosely planned, it was the people I met along the way who made it. This book belongs to all those people, as it is from their stories, lives, and recipes that I began to spin the fabric of it.

In Estonia, Meelike Naris organized meetings with local food producers and even came along as our translator—thank you, Meelike, for your warmth and your time. I hope you come to visit us soon! Thank you also to Mirjam Pikkmets, and Kaja and Urmas Kivisalu, for sharing your food stories.

In Riga, Linda Mazure was a massive help in my quest for culinary knowledge—thank you for sharing your food expertise, Linda. Madara Stella, thank you for inviting me into your home and feeding me such delicious modern Latvian food—it was a magical evening, and I believe your son is one to watch in the world of Baltic cuisine ...

In Lithuania, my biggest thanks go to Greta Žilytė, for sharing her recipes and childhood memories.

There are so many other people who contributed to this book, some of whom I met only briefly and whose names I don't even know, so I would like to extend my thanks to the people of the Baltics, for their generosity of spirit. Thank you also to everyone who shared their Baltic tips and recommendations prior to my research trip.

At home, I am very grateful for the support of my family and friends, especially my mom, Teresa Zakrzewska, who is always on hand to help, and my mom-in-law, Patricia Salazar, who is equally ready to share her knowledge and expertise. And last but by no means least, thank you, Olia Hercules, for your kind words of endorsement.

✖

First published in 2021 by

INTERLINK BOOKS
An imprint of Interlink Publishing Group, Inc.
46 Crosby Street
Northampton, Massachusetts 01060
www.interlinkbooks.com

Published simultaneously in the UK and Australia by Murdoch Books,
an imprint of Allen & Unwin

Publisher: Corinne Roberts
American edition publisher: Michel Moushabeck
Editorial manager: Justin Wolfers
Design manager and design: Vivien Valk
Project editor: Alison Cowan
American edition editor: Leyla Moushabeck
Food photography: Ola O. Smit
Food styling: Samantha Dixon and Kylee Newton
Props styling: Anna Wilkins
Travel photography: Yasin Salazar
Image on cover, title and chapter pages: Ashkan Forouzani on UnSplash
Patterns on cover and chapter pages adapted from images from istock.com
Production director: Lou Playfair

Library of Congress Cataloging-in-Publication Data available
ISBN 978-1-62371-900-5

Color reproduction by Splitting Image Color Studio Pty Ltd, Clayton, Victoria
Printed by C & C Offset Printing Co. Ltd., China

For our complete catalog, visit our website at
www.interlinkbooks.com or e-mail: sales@interlinkbooks.com

SAFETY NOTE
The ferment, pickle, curing, and preserve recipes in this book use traditional methods, passed down through generations. They have been updated for a modern kitchen, however since safety practices can differ regionally according to local risk factors, it is best to review the guidelines outlined by the National Center for Home Food Preservation before you start: https://nchfp.uga.edu/how/can_home.html.